IN SEARCH OF YOURSELF

Moving Forward

JANET DIAN

Illustrated by Lena Hardt

Expansions Publishing Company, Inc.
P. O. Box 1360
Ellensburg, WA   98926

Other books by Janet Dian—
In Search Of Yourself: The Beginning

IN SEARCH OF YOURSELF: Moving Forward. Text copyright © 1991 by
Janet Dian. Artwork copyright © 1991 by Lena Hardt. All rights reserved.
Printed in the United States of America. No part of this book may be used or
reproduced in any manner whatsoever without written permission except in
the case of brief quotations embodied in critical articles and reviews. For
information contact Expansions Publishing Company, Inc., P.O. Box 1360,
Ellensburg, WA 98926 U.S.A.

Library of Congress Catalog Card Number: 91-71002

ISBN 0-9626446-1-7

Publisher's Cataloging in Publication

Dian, Janet
    In search of yourself : moving forward / Janet Dian. --
    p. cm. -- (Self-healing through self-awareness ; book 2)
    Includes index.
    ISBN 0-9626446-1-7

    1. Metaphysics.   2. Self-realization.   3. Parapsychology.
I. Title. II. Series.

BP605.N48   133
                                      QBI91-424

A
SERIES
ON
SELF-HEALING
THROUGH
SELF-AWARENESS

Book 2

To all of you who responded
so enthusiastically to my first book.

CONTENTS

INTRODUCTION

Dear Friends,

"You make everything sound so simple and easy to understand!" is the most frequent comment I receive. Then, in the next breath, I am often excitedly asked, "How long will it all take?". This always makes me smile. I know exactly how you feel. It is exciting to find tools and principles that make immediate positive changes in your life.

At this point, you might compare yourself to a novice ice-skater. My first book presented the basic techniques. You are on the ice and you know how to skate. Book 2 presents techniques that will move you into the intermediate position. How long it takes to get there is entirely up to you. Jumps and spins take practice. As with anything, the more you practice the easier it all becomes.

My journey has taught me that the learning never ends. It only gets deeper and more interesting. And, that good can always get better. Wherever you are on your path, there is always an impetus for growth.

"Moving Forward" continues the journey that you started in Book 1. It guides you further along your unique path to your inner self, deeper into the knowledge that unlocks your personal doors.

This series of books is designed to grow with you. Each time you read them, you will find something new. As you change, the meaning of the passages deepens to meet your new level of understanding. Use the books as references. Pick one up any time that you have the inclination. Open it up and read a little. Any page, any chapter. Work with one principle or a part of one. Then work with another one or two.

Book 2 teaches you to appreciate the experiences in your life, whatever they may be. You will never pass through this part of your journey again in the same way, with the same knowledge, with the same people. Your journey is your personal pilgrimage in search of yourself—in search of your true identity.

Enjoy the process of "Moving Forward".

Janet Dian

UNRAVELING THE MYSTERIES

Imagine yourself the guest of honor at a party. There are five wrapped gifts on the table in front of you. Each one for you, but there is one catch. You can only open one gift every hour. Thus begins an evening of fun, intrigue, and, yes, mystery!

Opening the gifts over a period of time extends the excitement. The wait intensifies the entertainment. The anticipation of what is inside adds to the intrigue. Opening those gifts is like solving your own tiny mystery!

People Enjoy Mystery

People enjoy mystery. Mystery keeps you curious and entertained. Mystery teases you to solve the unknown. It is taunting with promises of secrets yet unrevealed.

Mystery has kept people entertained since time began. It has always challenged people to answer basic fundamental life questions, such as:

What shape is the earth?

What causes the sky to rain?

Where does the sun go during the night?

Where does the moon go during the day?

Does the sun orbit around the moon?

17

At one time these were very profound questions that stimulated debate and controversy. People devoted lifetimes to answering these questions. Today the answers are taken for granted. As with all things, the controversy faded as the mystery has faded.

All Knowledge Already Exists

All knowledge already exists. There is only one pool of knowledge. It just sits there, waiting to be "discovered".

Electricity existed before humankind discovered it. Fire existed before it was discovered. The transmission of sound waves through radio, telephone, and television existed before it was manifested into this dimension. The mystery for humankind was to find the clues that would bring that information forward into the collective conscious mind.

The *challenge* of unraveling the mysteries teaches people. Electricity itself is not mysterious, nor is fire, nor is the transmission of sound waves. A specific set of questions had to be asked in order to open the doors to that knowledge.

The explorers of human thought opened those doors through the process of trial and error. They found the correct combination of questions that allowed them to access that deeper knowledge. They did not find "new" knowledge. They tapped into existing knowledge, adding the perspective of known knowledge.

The Correct Combination Of Questions

Every person is in the middle of his/her own private mystery. Each individual must find the correct combination of questions that will unravel his/her own personal puzzle. A set of questions must be developed that leads into untapped knowledge. In turn, expanding upon those questions takes one into deeper knowledge. This continues to be a lifelong process of questions and answers, trial and error. Think of this in terms of opening a combination lock. No matter how many numbers you turn to, the lock will not open until *all* the correct numbers are known in the correct order.

The Mysteries Are For You

The mysteries are there for your entertainment, enjoyment, and fulfillment. You already have all the clues you need. You simply work with those clues until they give order and meaning to your particular mystery.

In the same way, a crossword puzzle contains all of its own answers. It comes with clues, including the number of letters per word. Each correct word is an additional clue for the next word. An "et" here or a "ra" there may not tell you anything for the moment. But each is a clue that leads to another question. The correct combination of questions leads into the correct answer. Eventually, the "et's" and "ra's" make sense. And, finally, the puzzle is finished.

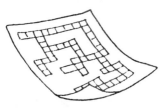

You Are A Mystery In Miniature

As a microcosm of the macrocosm, you are a mystery in miniature. You need the correct combination of questions that takes you into your very own answers. Solving the pieces to your own puzzle automatically begins to solve the grand mystery. The same rules apply to each. However, much like your own life, those answers come in bits and pieces.

Eventually, you will have the big picture. But for now, take the pieces that you are given. No matter how small, file them away for later use. Remember, the entertainment is in the process of solving the mystery. The answer is the prize for working the process correctly.

Life itself is open, simple, and clean. People are the ones who surround it with mystery and intrigue. The answers are already there. Sometimes it is so simple that it only appears complex.

Learn From The Soaps

Soap operas are wonderful examples of how easy it is to complicate life's simple situations. The process of how people set their own life circumstances in motion are blatantly detailed in "soaps". But nonetheless, they are good examples of how situations can quickly become complicated and messy.

Soap operas often reflect real life in their own exaggerated way. Use them as a study tool. Ask yourself if they reflect your life. If you have an adverse reaction to soap operas, search for deeper meaning. It may mean that they can teach you! Remember, only when your reaction to a situation is neutral are you really finished with it.

Horizontal/Vertical Experiences

The mysteries will unravel even faster when you choose vertical experiences over horizontal ones.

Definition:

Vertical experiences pull you *up* into *new* growth.

Horizontal experiences pull you *out* into *similar* growth.

For example, say you are vice president of a company. Another company offers you a job with the same title and level of responsibility. This move is a horizontal one. Going from company to company as vice president brings the same types of experiences. Although each vice presidency will vary somewhat, the general job description remains the same.

However, a move from vice president to president to chief executive officer is vertical growth. Each position moves you upward in your learning experiences. Each step up broadens your knowledge. Each time you have learned the previous position well in order to be offered the next vertical position.

Everyone has many horizontal experiences. You may belong to six local service organizations. If they bring you the same types of experiences, they are horizontal experiences. However, belonging to a local, county, and state service organization may provide vertical experiences.

Consider the following analogy. Visualize a washcloth and label it "experience". Wring it until it is as dry as possible. Now think of each personal experience as that washcloth. Wring it dry for every drop of knowledge that it holds. Treating every experience in this way successfully establishes vertical growth.

Once you make a conscious decision to grow vertically, you may be surprised at the acceleration of your growth rate. You extract so much knowledge from each experience that you have fewer of the same types of experiences. This means you now have more correct combinations of questions that will move you faster into continually deeper levels of inner knowledge.

Understand your microcosm first. Know that it is the secret to understanding the macrocosm. As your personal mystery unravels, rules to the deeper mysteries automatically reveal themselves.

YOUR PERSONAL PUZZLE

There are very basic rules to follow when solving your own personal puzzle. The first one is easy to overlook because it sounds so simple—it is called observation.

All you have to do is learn to observe. You express who you are just by being. Your body language, tone of voice, colors you choose to wear, and home all reflect what is happening inside of yourself. Even the people that you choose to have in your life reflect you. These reflections teach you about yourself when you let them. But when you hurry through life you may have a tendency to overlook these key clues.

Organize Your Life Into Moments

Put the process in motion by slowing down long enough to allow each moment equal importance. This organizes your life into moments that you can observe and evaluate. A moment is a very small fraction of time that you can deal with *right now*. Past years, months, weeks, and days all began in a moment. Organizing your moments automatically organizes your life.

For example, group happy moments together. Group peaceful moments together. Group satisfied moments together. Observe them, looking for the common action that led to these positive moments. Once you know, you can repeat those same types of moments in conscious awareness.

This allows you to consciously bring more happy, peaceful, satisfied, etc., moments into your life.

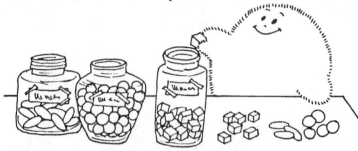

In the same way, group your negative moments together. A significant other puts you down, then a friend rejects you. The pharmacist at the local drugstore verbally abuses you. Group these moments together. You had a common action that led to these similar results. Recall the previous moments to find the common action.

You may not be able to find the common action from only three incidents. That is okay. Continue to group similar moments together. Eventually, the common action will become very obvious. This may take a long time, or it may happen very quickly.

Once you have a group of similar moments, you are on your way. Continue to observe them. Evaluate them for the similar actions that lead to similar results. With this knowledge, you can create less or more of any type of moment that you desire.

View Your Life With Objectivity

The interesting part of observing is learning to do it objectively, without judgment or criticism of self. This increases the intrigue and challenge. As the saying goes, "it is easier to solve someone else's problems than your own". That is because it is easier to step back and view another's life with objectivity.

Learn to be an objective observer of your own life. This means withdrawing the emotional involvement from your moments in order to make accurate evaluations. You need a clear picture of your life to make honest assessments of where you are and where you want to go. Become the subject of your very own study.

Work From Your Center

You need a home base from which to work. You need a place that is safe and comfortable. A place that you can take with you wherever you go. That place is your center. You began building it in Book 1 in the chapter, "Into the Silence".

Breathe yourself into it any time that you feel scattered or uncomfortable. Will yourself into your center. Feel the deep inner connection to your Oversoul and God. Feel the strength that is yours to claim. Know that as long as you remain in your center, you are safe. You can look at anything that you choose to express knowing that it is your action, but it is not you. You are separate from your actions. You are the actor/actress on the stage.

You can make any decision that you want while you are in your center. But whatever you choose to express, either positive or negative, do it in conscious awareness. If you

27

want to keep negative moments in your life, do not hide this decision from yourself. Be honest. Be negative, but do it in awareness. Then observe the consequences of those moments. Continue to evaluate what you want in your life and why.

You may not be ready to let go of the negative moments. This is perfectly acceptable. However, do acknowledge their existence as well as your role in maintaining them. If you choose to keep them, then grow by allowing them to teach you. When the time comes, you will let them go.

To start the process, will yourself into your center. Watch your actions and words as though it were the very first time that you have ever met this person that you call yourself. Start playing the role of an objective observer with these questions:

What is your opinion of this person?

Is this person someone that you would like to know?

Would you enjoy his/her company?

What is the tone of his/her voice?

What kind of emotions does he/she express, and when?

How does he/she treat his/her body?

How does he/she treat his/her material world?

How does he/she interact with other people?

Become Your Own Video Camera

Become your own video camera that is in the process of recording you only for the purpose of evaluation. Do not judge or criticize. Only observe and gather data to get an accurate, unbiased look at your moments.

Observe yourself being happy, calm, peaceful, hard-working, punctual, easy-going; sad, angry, irritated, lazy, late, up-tight.

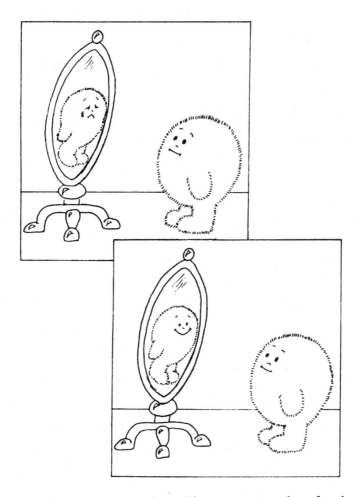

The list can go on and on. These are examples of actions that are separate from you. As you observe, ask yourself these questions:

What do I think of these actions?

Do I want more or less of these types of actions in my life?

Do I like myself when I act like this?

How do other people respond to me when I act like this?

How important are these types of actions to me?

Am I willing to let any of them go?

Use this information to make accurate decisions about which types of moments you want to keep and which ones you no longer need. As you gather the data, pass them up the channel that connects you to your Oversoul. Feel the evaluations come down the channel. This moves your energy vertically, preparing you for vertical growth. Releasing what you already know further opens the doors to inner knowledge.

When you first start observing yourself, it may be difficult to watch yourself express emotions and actions that you would rather not see.

Your first reaction may be to judge and criticize. You most likely have established vibratory imprints of self-criticism and self-judgment. It took time to build them; it takes time to dismantle them.

Releasing Judgment Of Self

Self-criticism and self-judgment are a natural part of the process. You may even find yourself criticizing and judging yourself because you are criticizing and judging yourself! If you do, merely acknowledge your actions in an objective way. For instance, you could say:

"Here I go, criticizing and judging myself again. I release those criticisms and judgments up to my Oversoul. In return, I ask for understanding of my actions. I also ask for alternative avenues of action to replace the ones that I am in the process of releasing."

You are *in the process* of learning how to be non-critical and non-judgmental of self. Although that is your goal, you are not there yet. You are just now learning the necessary steps to get there. It does not make sense to chastise yourself for something that you do not yet know how to do. Simply acknowledge that you are being critical and judgmental. Release those feelings up to your Oversoul. Move into the observing stage as best as you can.

Any new action feels awkward at first. With practice, observing yourself objectively becomes easier. The old vibratory imprint weakens while the new imprint gains strength.

Remember to observe from your center. Also remember that your emotions and actions are separate from you. They are not you; they cannot consume you. Remain in your center instead of fully participating in a no-longer-desired behavior pattern. As you separate yourself from these emotions and actions, they become easier to watch. As a result your evaluations become more accurate.

All information that you gather about yourself is equally important. Negative information tells you about your weak areas. Positive information denotes your strengths. Use the positive to buttress your weak areas. Take a moment to thank your Oversoul for the people and experiences that bring those weak areas to your attention. Without them, you would not be aware of your weaknesses.

Make Changes Now

Because you are in a constant state of growth, everything that goes into you eventually moves out of you. Experiences come into your life from your Oversoul, leaving a vibratory imprint. Sooner or later, the vibratory imprint will return to your Oversoul. Take the initiative to move it out in conscious awareness.

Objective observing gives you the opportunity to release the negatives in conscious awareness. Your alternative may be to have it forced out of you at some later point in time. This is your chance to make changes now in the least uncomfortable way possible.

The observing process shows you that you have a preconceived idea of who you are, what you express, and how you choose to express it. Objective observing provides the opportunity to find out if who you are really matches that picture.

You may be surprised at the differences in the illusions that you have versus the reality of what is. You may find that there are parts of yourself that are not as "bad" as you thought.

You may also find that there are parts that are not as "wonderful" as you thought. Do your best to remain as objective as possible, no matter what you discover. Change your attitude—

from

"Oh no, here I go again!"

to

"Oh boy, here I grow again!"

Always acknowledge that you are where you are supposed to be with the tools and experiences that you have. Objective observing means stating the facts—what does or does not exist:

I am irritated.

She irritates me.

The situation irritates me.

The above examples only acknowledge fact. There is no criticism or judgment involved. Once you state the facts, then you can evaluate, and move from there. Go slowly, without undue pressure on yourself. Continue moving forward as best as you can.

Let Others Teach You

As you observe yourself moment by moment, you become more aware of why you act and react the way that you do. This in turn clarifies others' actions and reactions toward you. Remember, you express who you are just by being.

Others react to that expression, whether they are aware of it or not. They react to your body language, tone of voice, colors you choose to wear, and the contents of your aura. They process this information very quickly on an unconscious level of awareness, usually unaware of its effect upon them.

Act In Conscious Awareness

Slowing down the process allows you to act in conscious awareness. You become aware of everything that you choose to project, moment by moment. This means you make conscious decisions about the colors you wear, words you speak, tone of voice, gestures, and what you keep in your aura.

Now you can understand why people react to you as they do. If their reactions disturb you, ask these questions:

What can I change so that others react to me differently?

Which one of my qualities are they showing me?

What are they teaching me about myself?

The people that you choose to have around you reflect who you are. If you do not like their actions, then it is your puzzle to find out what *you* can change within to change that reflection.

An Objective Observer

An objective observer sees, hears, touches, tastes, and smells with great acuity. The senses heighten as you process all available information. Your analysis of any given moment becomes very accurate.

Over time, self-observations become less judgmental and critical. It becomes easier to release undesired behavior with less attachment to your actions. You develop a softer, gentler attitude toward yourself as you release the harsh judge. It is replaced with understanding and compassion for self. In turn, others reflect that softer, gentler attitude back to you.

As an objective observer, you now have a method to sort and organize your life. Do it moment by moment, slowly and methodically. Group similar moments with similar moments. Through observation, identify the similar action that led to similar results. Decide in conscious awareness the types of moments you want in your life. And make conscious decisions of how you want to put them there.

WHAT DID YOU SAY?

Inner listening is very simple. The secret is to start by listening to yourself. Listen objectively, without judgment or criticism. Listen only for the purpose of gathering data and making evaluations.

Breathe yourself into your center, and observe yourself as the objective listener. For instance, listen to the tone of your voice. Ask yourself, is it:

pleasant?

gentle?

kind?

calm?

harsh?

overbearing?

sharp?

too quiet?

too loud?

What does your tone express?

contentment?

peacefulness?

happiness?

understanding?

anger?

resentment?

sadness?

insecurity?

guilt?

Choose Empowering Words

Pay attention to the words that you choose. If you listen to them, they will teach you about your state of inner being. Listen for phrases that weaken body, mind, or spirit. Choose to release the need for words that do not affirm the positive in your life.

Listen to the words that you choose:

Do they affirm the positive or negative in your life?

For example:

I am trying to learn how to improve myself.
Trying is not the same as doing.

I am afraid that I am going to be late.
This is a statement of inner being.

I can't afford not to go to class.
Are you holding back prosperity with this phrase?

I am sick and tired of hearing you complain.
What does this phrase contribute to your health?

I can't stand it.
> Back, feet, or legs giving you any problem?

I hate being late.
> Do you hate?

I don't deserve this wonderful surprise.
> What *do* you deserve?

The words that you have chosen for many years, perhaps many lifetimes, have set the patterns into motion that you live today. The words that you chose yesterday, a few minutes ago, set up the experiences of today, of this moment.

Match Words With Feelings

Do your words match what you feel inside?

> Do your words say that you are happy when you truly are not?

> Do you say that one thing frustrates you when it is really something else?

> Do you complain about your current circumstances when there is a part of you that enjoys it?

Observe Body Language

Observe your body language as you speak:

> What gestures do you make?

> When do you make them?

> Do your gestures match your words and/or inner feelings?

Your body language tells you about yourself. On some level of awareness, it also tells others about you. When words match tone of voice, feelings, and body language, they convey a much stronger and clearer message.

Talking Without Listening

It is easy to talk without really listening to yourself. Words sometimes just tumble out while your mind is wandering elsewhere. People react to the lack of attention that you pay to your own words. Why should they listen to you if you do not care enough to listen to yourself?

Are you the only one participating in the conversation? Are you:

rambling?

repeating the same story?

bored with your own conversation?

getting too personal?

offering unwanted advice?

talking about something that the other person cares nothing about?

Remember, gather the data for evaluation purposes only. If you start judging or criticizing yourself, simply acknowledge what you are doing. Then pass those feelings on up to your Oversoul.

Objectively Listen

Because the outer always reflects the inner, objectively listen to others when they speak. Their tone of voice, words that they choose, and body language all reflect some part of you—past, present, or future.

Objectively listen and let the other person teach you. Too often, people actively engage in talking to themselves instead of conversing with each other. While one is speaking, the other is busy thinking about what he/she will say next. When you think about the conversation later, it is much easier to recall what you said, how you said it, and how clever you were. It is much more difficult to recall what the other person said.

Do not listen to judge or criticize, but to let others reflect yourself back to you. If they ramble consistently, you had better check yourself for the same quality. If they are boring, then ask yourself to notice when you are boring. If they are judgmental or critical, look to see where you might be judgmental or critical.

Objectively listen to others. Use the same list of questions that you apply to yourself. Then use that knowledge to objectively listen to yourself.

Whenever anyone speaks to you, there is a reason. They take time to show you something about yourself. Therefore, evaluate everything that is spoken to you for validity. Even words spoken in anger might force you to face an area of yourself that you have been avoiding. When someone is very angry with you, it catches your attention. Those same words spoken in kindness might not be heard.

Always evaluate any accusations, judgments, criticisms, observations, or off-handed comments. Perhaps they are valid remarks. Or perhaps this is a chance for you to stand up for yourself. Tell your Oversoul that you will listen as long as these experiences are explained to your satisfaction.

Selective Listening

Sometimes on an unconscious level of awareness you pick and choose what you want to hear. This is selective listening. Selective listening occurs when you hear only what you *want* to hear. What you decide to listen to and retain usually perpetuates your self-illusions.

These illusions can be either positive or negative. In your mind, you have a picture of who you are. If what you hear does not match that picture, you may not retain any of that conversation.

For instance, someone may pay you a compliment that you do not think you deserve. You may not really hear or remember it because you do not think that it is valid. Or, suppose six people compliment a project that you feel good about. Then one person makes a casual off-handed remark that indicates the project is inferior.

You may choose to remember that remark if you retain an illusion of low self-worth. You can choose to use that comment to nurture your illusions. Or, you can choose to use it as a growth tool. The person who spoke those words provided a test for you. Pull yourself into your center. Use that opportunity as a chance to acknowledge your self-worth.

Listen Through Your Oversoul

Listen to others through your Oversoul. As they speak, ask your Oversoul to explain their words to you. Push your energy up through the channel that connects you with your Oversoul. Ask your Oversoul:

What is the feeling behind the words?

What is this person *really* saying to me?

What does this person *really* want to know from me?

Direct the energy of your words up through your Oversoul. Then, ask your Oversoul to direct both your spoken and unspoken words.

Levels Of Listening

Objective listening automatically takes you deeper inside. It moves you into new levels of inner awareness. As a natural part of the process, you hear with greater clarity. Your mind becomes more focused and directed.

The following are different ways one listens:

Words

Feelings

Energy

Color

Vibration

Words

People most often associate listening with words. Words on the outer levels are important. They direct your attention, giving you a reference point for communication. However, as you move into the deeper levels of listening, you find that there are no words. Words as you commonly think of them are not always necessary.

Feelings

Behind the words are feelings. Feelings come first. Words are then attached to explain those feelings.

Observe people who grope for the "right" words to explain their experiences. They often first make a series of hand gestures that depict feelings. They may even spit and stutter a little as they work to find those "right" words.

When this occurs take the opportunity to listen through your Oversoul. Ask your Oversoul to explain the feelings before they become spoken words. This helps you connect with the level of feeling.

As you practice, others may label you "psychic". But all you are doing is objectively listening to the feelings that are already present. You are not doing anything unusual or strange. You are only aware of what exists *right now.* Your Oversoul explains your evaluations.

As an added thought, recognize that you are in the process of moving beyond psychic, or personal energy. When you allow others to label you psychic, they confine you to that level. Using universal energy takes you into the level of "knowing by knowing". Keep true to your goal without stopping in the process.

Energy

Feelings are comprised of energy. They have form and consistency. Listen to the energy that you use behind the words that you speak. Feel it, passing those feelings up to your Oversoul. Using the following sample questions, ask your Oversoul to direct your learning:

Is the energy—

clear?

muddy?

Does the energy have—

> solidity?
>
> strength?
>
> holes?
>
> webs?

What kind of weight does the energy have—

> horizontal weight?
>
> vertical weight?

The feel of the energy behind the words tells many things. When you "puff" up your stories, that is exactly what happens to your energy. It comes out of your mouth in puffs and floats away.

When you do not know what you are talking about the energy is full of holes. Muddy energy may contain a lie. Boring energy feels horizontal. On the other hand, truth feels strong, solid, and clear.

Color

The psychic energy with which people speak has color. The feeling behind the words and combination of words create wave lengths of color.

You may not be able to see the colors with your physical eyes, but you can feel them. Begin to associate words, feelings, and energy with color. Feel when they match, keeping in mind that all color has both positive and negative qualities.

Read through the following examples. Observe the feelings while visualizing the hue of the colors used in each example.

Negative: His yellow streak was showing.

Positive: He had a golden moment.

Negative: She was so mad she saw red.

Positive: She had a red-letter day.

Negative: He is green with jealousy.

Positive: He has a green thumb.

Recognize that the negative statements have a heavy feeling while the positive statements have a light feeling. Negative hues tend to be dark and cloudy. Positive ones tend to be lighter and clearer.

Objectively listen, feeling the color of your own words. Ask your Oversoul to direct the learning process with the following questions:

What color are my words?

—a clear color?
—a muddy color?

Is it important that I know?

The energy and colors of a conversation change as subjects change. Communication with others is most effective when you both speak in the same color. When you speak in orange and the other person speaks in blue, you have difficulty communicating. It is important to communicate on the "same wave length".

As you converse, visualize what you think the colors might be. Keep passing your observations up to your Oversoul while asking these questions:

> Does the color of my words match the color of his/her words?
>
> Do I want the colors to match?
> (Changing the color of your words changes the conversation.)
>
> Am I getting my point across?
> (Ask your Oversoul to match the colors for you.)

Everyone reacts to the color of words on some level of awareness. If someone chooses to take an ego trip at your expense, you may react to the sharpness of his/her bright orange words. To end the conversation, speak to him/her in a different color. If it is your boss, you may choose to speak back in orange, allowing the ego-boosting conversation to continue!

Right now, merely be aware that color is a function of listening. When you *need* to understand, you will.

Vibration

The next level of listening is vibration. The vibratory imprints of past experiences surround every person. These vibratory imprints contain your past, present, and the future that you are in the process of creating. As your objective listening skills develop, tune into your own vibratory imprints. Listen to them. They will relate whatever events your Oversoul wishes you to know.

Listen to your vibratory imprints during meditation. Breathe yourself into your center. Ask your Oversoul to tell you who and what you are. Tell your Oversoul to prepare you for the answers.

As you move into ever-deeper levels of inner listening, let your Oversoul teach you. It will always show you whatever you *need* to know. This is different from what you might *want* to know. Trust the wisdom of your Oversoul.

Inner Listening

The process of inner listening begins in the present. Tone of voice, words that you choose, and body language are all known knowledge. Study what you have in front of you *right now.* Understanding known knowledge leads you into your own previously untapped knowledge.

Never overlook the simplicity of the beginning point. Appreciate what you have instead of criticizing and/or judging yourself for what you do not have. When you appreciate your present moment, it will teach you. It will provide the answers *and* the questions that will move you deeper inside of yourself, closer to who you really are.

MOVING FORWARD

As you organize and observe your moments, you have some decisions to make:

Which actions do I want to keep?

Which actions am I ready to discard?

How do I make those decisions?

And finally, the most important question of all:

How do I feel about change?

Change is one of those processes that is often easier to talk about than to implement.

Change means—

moving out of the status quo.

moving out of your comfort zone and into unfamiliar territory.

actively pursuing new avenues of action.

putting yourself and your capabilities on the line.

taking risks.

All of the above means that at some point you may feel awkward, insecure, foolish, and/or inadequate. Even change that you recognize as positive can be a threat. You can no longer rely on old habit responses to get you through new challenges. It may be difficult to look for the adventure in a new experience when you feel the discomfort that an unfamiliar one brings.

Are you willing to—

be flexible?

release the old?

move through your fears?

accept and implement the new?

assume responsibility for deeper knowledge?

Each person can only hold a given number of experiences. You can choose to hold onto the old, familiar ones. Or, you

can choose to release them. Releasing them allows new experiences rich with knowledge to enter your life.

Your search for self is a process of moving through the known into the unknown. Moving into the unknown means accessing different knowledge. This changes you, your reactions, and your outer world's reactions. This also brings greater responsibility.

Responsibility

What are you going to do with your "new" knowledge? Are you going to use it to help others or manipulate them? To understand or criticize? To progress on your journey or impress others? Responsibility comes with knowledge. A deeper awareness of the mysteries of life makes you more accountable for your actions.

Compare this to the laws of society. A child who takes a candy bar without paying may not realize that society calls this stealing. When caught, the act may only warrant a firm explanation. But a child who takes a candy bar with the knowledge that it is stealing will be dealt with with greater severity.

As further explanation, pretend that you tap into knowledge that allows you to heal everyone you touch. Does this give you permission to run through all the hospitals healing everyone you see?

This would probably give you a great feeling of self-importance. People everywhere would beg for your attention. Is this your goal? Where would this put you on your path? Just because you *can* do something, does that give you permission to do it indiscriminately?

All knowledge brings responsibility. With illness comes lessons. If you take away illness indiscriminately, you may take away the only chance some people have to learn. However, there may be others your Oversoul will direct you to heal. They have learned their lessons. They just need a little help moving into their next level of awareness. Work with your Oversoul. Ask your Oversoul to give you the wisdom to correctly use whatever knowledge is revealed to you.

Attitude Is Important

Your attitude toward change is important. Your objective observations and listening skills teach you about yourself with honesty. Be honest with yourself about what you really *want* to change.

Identify something that you would like to change. Start the process by asking the following questions:

Do I really *want* to change it?

or

Do I just think that I *should* change it?

There is a difference. For example, do you really *want* to give up smoking? Or do you just think that you *should?* If you truly *do not want* to give it up, why spend time fighting against yourself? Without criticism or judgment of self, simply acknowledge that for now you like to smoke. When the time is right, you will give it up. For now, choose something else. Focus your energy on something that you *want* to change.

An Exchange With Change

Next, recognize that there is always an exchange with change.

Consider these examples:

You must give up money to purchase a sofa.

You must give up the old sofa to make room for the new one.

You must give up sickness along with its perks, for health.

You must give up anger, bitterness, and resentment for peace of mind.

No matter what you decide to change, you will always give up something in exchange. This may be a major factor in your decision to make changes. Ask the following questions:

What will I lose by changing?

What will I gain by changing?

Decide if what you will gain outweighs what you will lose. If any part of you does not want to let go, acknowledge it. Then pass those feelings on up to your Oversoul. Move forward with your change.

Three Steps To Change

There are three basic steps to change:

Trying

The first step is *trying*. The old vibratory imprint is still very strong. It seems to have a mind of its own. It pulls you the moment you look the other direction.

You are *trying* to loosen its strength. You are *trying* to establish a new imprint, but it is still very young and weak. Affirmations are extremely important at this time. They establish new feelings in your aura. Use them often to continually strengthen the new imprint.

Prepare yourself to be pulled back into the old vibratory imprint. Do not criticize yourself when this happens. Observe that it is happening and realize that this is a natural part of the process of change. Evaluate how you can act differently the next time. Release all of your feelings up to your Oversoul.

Becoming

The next step in the process is *becoming*. The old vibratory imprint is weakening. You release more of it up to your Oversoul. Affirmations are still important, but not as mandatory. The new vibratory imprint is strengthening.

This is a transition period. You may find yourself in a push-me, pull-me situation, not totally comfortable with the new, yet no longer comfortable with the old. You may even feel like giving up the change. Yet, deep down you know that you cannot go back.

During this stage, the old vibratory imprint pulls you back less often. You still fall into it from time to time, but it is losing its strength.

Being

The last and final step is *being*. The old vibratory imprint is totally broken up and released to your Oversoul. The new vibratory imprint is strong and established. It functions in accordance with the way that you built it. Affirmations are no longer necessary. You no longer have to *try*. You just *are*. The new vibratory imprint is expressed in the way you speak, your mannerisms, and your overall attitudes.

Creative Thinking

Sometimes after identifying a change that you really *want* to make, you may have difficulty deciding how to make it. Your mind may seem locked into one pattern of behavior. It may run you around in circles *trying* to find a new solution to an old situation.

You may need some practice in the area of creative thinking. Do this by stimulating new areas of your brain to induce new methods of thinking. Start small and be successful. Begin the process simply by doing very ordinary tasks in extraordinary ways. This breaks up old habit responses that result from old vibratory imprints. This also stimulates new areas of your brain. You could:

Wear your watch on the "other" arm.

Sleep on the "other" side of the bed.

Eat with your "other" hand.

Drink your morning coffee from a different cup.

Drive to work using a different route.

Park in a different parking space.

Anything that breaks up regular routines forces you to think differently. New brain cells are stimulated into action. These simple activities allow new avenues of action to filter into your conscious mind.

Creative thinking sets the stage for change. These small changes allow you to associate new feelings with success. Thus you gain confidence to attempt larger, more significant changes.

The thought of a major change can sometimes be overwhelming. You may procrastinate so long that you never begin. Fear of failure (or of success!) leads you to do nothing.

However, starting in the beginning establishes a new vibratory imprint that says:

Change is possible.

Change is acceptable.

Change can be fun and exciting.

Start small, and feel good about your progress. Take one step at a time. If one step is too threatening, then take a half-step, or a quarter-step. Change in a way that is comfortable for you.

Your Change May Threaten Others

Your change may threaten others. As you change, others must change their reactions to you. Any change you make automatically forces them out of their comfort zones and into unfamiliar territory.

Suddenly, they may find themselves in new growth patterns that they may not be consciously prepared to accept. Because this takes them out of their status quo, they may try to sabotage your change. This might be a conscious or unconscious reaction.

For instance, you finally decide to lose that extra weight. You start a strict diet, thinking your family and friends will be thrilled. As you lose the weight, your spouse begins to feel very insecure. He/she wonders if he/she will remain the most important person in your life. He/she starts tempting you with all your favorite foods.

Your best friend becomes jealous because he/she thinks that you look better than he/she does. Your friendship becomes strained and uncomfortable. Both your spouse and friend are rebelling against your very positive change. They may not consciously be aware that your change causes their insecurities to surface.

For this reason, it is always important to share your plans with others on the inner levels. Explain to them through their Oversouls what changes you are in the process of making and why. Explain fears and frustrations, while acknowledging their right to be afraid. Know that on some level they realize that your change means their change.

Remember, you will always have people around you who best reflect you to yourself. Either they must change to continue that reflection, or drop out of your life. Respect their struggles.

All You Have Is A Thought

A decision to change begins with a thought. The success of your change depends upon the strength of that thought. Thoughts create the energy that moves you into and through a change.

Your original thought is a seed of energy. Every time you think about making the change, you produce similar thoughts. These similar thoughts are drawn to that energy seed. This process gathers "thought" energy.

When you collect enough "thought" energy, change can begin. However, it is possible to lose that energy if you:

Speak too soon.

or

Act too soon.

Every time you speak, you disperse energy. Speaking too soon about a planned change weakens the seed. It must wait for more thoughts to regain its strength. Talking about a plan of action in its early stage of energy gathering weakens the plan. Continuing to talk about it may mean that enough energy may never accumulate to follow through with an action. You are probably familiar with the saying, "He's all talk and no action". This is why.

For this reason, speak very little about your plans. Advise others via the involved Oversouls, but keep as much "thought" energy as possible to yourself. Use it to accomplish your goals.

Accumulated energy can also be dispersed by acting too soon. Gather enough "thought" energy to propel you on through to your goals. Affirmations add energy to the seed thought. Reading books that enforce your goals also helps. Even the company that you keep strengthens the process. Be among people who pull you up into your potential.

Correct Timing

Determine the correct timing for action. Rely on what you know about feeling before you speak or act. When you speak or act too soon, remember the feeling. When you speak or act and everything flows smoothly, remember that feeling. These experiences build a data base that you can use for future reference.

Release the data base up to your Oversoul. Before speaking or acting, ask your Oversoul if this is the correct timing. Match what you want to do with the feeling coming back from your Oversoul. Your inner communications tell you when the timing is correct.

How Do I Feel About Change?

How you feel about change affects all the answers to all the questions that you will ask along your journey. Your capacity to change determines how deep within you will go.

Change means—

Growth.

Expansion.

Movement.

New and exciting experiences.

Embrace change. Enjoy the variety of experiences that it brings. Let it teach you about your depths yet unrevealed.

YOU HAVE A CHOICE

You choose your own words and actions. Other people or situations can only evoke behavior that already exists within you. No one can make you respond in any particular way unless you choose to do so.

Occasionally people get so locked into patterns of behavior that they forget that they have choices. You do not have to respond to the same situations in the same ways unless you make that choice. For instance:

Are you grumpy when you wake up in the morning?

Does mowing the lawn irritate you?

Do you resent cleaning the house?

Are you angry at the morning traffic?

Are you impatient with your children?

All of the above are examples of habit responses. You automatically feel a certain way. You automatically react to those feelings. You do not stop and question if you want those reactions in your life. You make your choices without thinking.

Definition:

A habit response is an established pattern of behavior that allows you to react to any given situation without thinking—whether physical or mental; positive, negative, or neutral.

Physical Habit Responses

Walking is an example of a physical habit response. Learning to walk is a difficult task for a child. Maintaining balance, shifting weight at just the right time, and avoiding collisions with objects takes all of a child's concentration.

Eventually, walking becomes a habit response. This habit response allows children to walk at will. It also frees them to talk, carry things, and eat while walking. An adult no longer has to think about how to walk. An adult just walks.

Mental Habit Responses

Mental habit responses develop in the same way. They also allow you to react without thinking. Your neighbor working in her yard makes you smile and say hello. Your son running through the house automatically makes you snap at him to slow down. You really do not put much thought into either activity. Having done it before, you most likely will do it again.

Habit Responses Are Comfortable

Habit responses are comfortable. They just sit there, waiting for you to use them. Habit responses are ready responses. They are tried-and-true courses of action. You know how you will react. You can predict how others will react.

Your neighbor smiles back and says hello. Your son momentarily slows down. Without interrupting your lifestyle, you have ready responses to familiar situations. For many situations, this is fine.

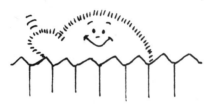

Old Habit Responses

In most instances habit responses start off very innocently. You use a course of action once and it works. The next time a similar situation arises you use it again. The next thing you know, you have a habit response. These habit responses serve a purpose for a time. They add efficiency to your life.

However, as you change you may forget to reprogram your habit responses. You may continue to rely on habit responses that are no longer appropriate. Accustomed to using them without thinking, you may fail to realize what you are doing and why.

Evaluate some of your own habit responses to determine if they are still useful. Think about situations that always evoke similar responses. Do you have a habit of speaking harshly? Do you have an underlying pattern of bitterness and resentment? If so, why? Where did it come from?

Do you have a habit of wringing your hands? Is this a sign of tension in other areas of your life? What can you do to relieve that tension?

Do you have a habit of being late? Is it because you are accustomed to getting attention in a negative way? Are you ready to let go of negative attention?

Do you have a habit of not liking your physical body? What part do you not like? When did you stop liking it and why? Is it time to let those feelings go?

You may be surprised at how often you react without knowing why. Words just pop out of your mouth. Actions just occur. Pay attention to what you do and why. Acknowledging and labeling your actions increases your ability to choose in conscious awareness.

Now ask yourself:

Could I react to these situations differently?

Do I want to?

Would my life be more pleasant?

Would I feel better about myself?

Taking the time to stop and think before you react makes room for options and choices. Even stopping and thinking after the fact is progress. At least you are aware of what you did. You can evaluate the situation and decide how you would like to react the next time. Eventually, you will stop and think before you react.

Habit responses exist whether you choose to use them or not. For this reason, it is important to identify and evaluate them. Release the ones that you no longer need up to your Oversoul.

Habit Responses Are Interconnected

Habit responses are often interconnected. Fear is a good example. You may have:

fear of heights.

fear of knives.

fear of airplanes.

fear of water.

fear that your children might hurt themselves.

fear that you might not finish in time.

fear of looking foolish.

fear that you are not good enough.

At first glance, all of these situations might appear to be very different. But reading through the list, you easily see that they all relate to the habit response of fear. Fear feeds upon fear; fear builds upon fear. These experiences are definitely interconnected.

Weakening fear any way possible weakens the habit response. Releasing fear of knives helps release any or all fears. This takes away energy from an already strong habit response.

Moving through fear instead of using fear as a reaction stops adding strength to your habit response. Changing your reaction to one fear creates a positive chain reaction until one day you will get on an airplane and suddenly notice you are no longer afraid. Fear dissipates itself from lack of nourishment.

Build New Habit Responses

Consciously build new habit responses that contain more desirable patterns of behavior. Use affirmations to help you. Affirmations create new feelings within, establishing a foundation for new patterns of behavior. Each time you affirm a positive habit response, you increase its strength. Eventually you automatically react in a positive way.

These new habit responses contain more desirable reactions that match your current level of development. They help redefine your life in a positive way. Consciously choose habit responses that affirm:

I speak gently.

I am healthy.

I am prosperous.

I have loving, comfortable relationships.

I appreciate all activities in my life.

I am peaceful and calm inside.

I am thankful for all that I have.

Release the habit responses that you no longer need. Choose to build new ones that recreate your life in a positive way. Remember, you have a choice.

MOVING THROUGH ILLUSION

Illusion is important. It allows you to play-act through life. After all, you are only an actor/actress on a stage in this grand illusion called "life". Before birth, you choose the role that you want to play. Then you choose the country, race, and parents that help create that role.

Your name, age, occupation, race, and religion are all part of your illusion. They describe a particular role at a particular moment in time and space.

As neutral energy, you exist beyond physical birth through physical death. Your physical body changes lifetime after lifetime. Yet *you* remain an evolutionizing constant. You encompass a time frame that equals infinity.

Expand Your Definition Of Self

The following questions may begin to move forward into your conscious mind as you expand your definition of self:

What experiences brought me to this point in time?

How did my thoughts, feelings, and attitudes develop?

What influenced and shaped me?

What strengthened me?

What weakened me?

What people were in my lives and why?

What other dimensions have I experienced?

These questions have a multitude of answers depending upon how deeply inside you take them. There are many layers of illusion, accumulated from this lifetime and others. These illusions have entertained and fascinated you for eons. They are a part of the process of God learning about God.

The deeper you go, the more layers you penetrate. Moving through layer upon layer of illusion brings you closer to reality. You are in the process of acquiring the necessary tools to move beyond illusion and into reality.

Exchange Illusion For Reality

Moving through illusion sounds easy on paper. However, remember there is always an exchange with change. If you give up illusion, what do you get in return? Reality.

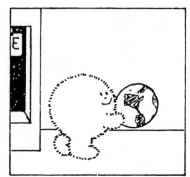

Illusion leaves the process open; the possibilities are endless. Reality states fact. This can be frightening. Moving through illusion into a layer of reality means new knowledge. New knowledge means responsibility and change. Many people do not progress when they realize this.

Illusion allows you to make up the answers to your own questions. Illusion is only limited by your imagination.

Knowing the answers moves you directly into reality. Reality is an entirely different matter.

To illustrate this point, think about this. You apply for a job that you really want. As long as you hear nothing, there is still a possibility that you will be hired. Even though the waiting is tedious, there is hope. However, with the answer comes reality. Either yes or no. There is no more illusion, only fact.

Take the shape of the earth as another example. At one time it was accepted as fact that the earth was flat. People speculated and discussed at great length about what lay beyond the edge. Theologians speculated that hell lay just over the edge. Artists painted pictures of the dragons and demons that they thought lived beyond the edge of the earth. The illusion of a flat earth provided entertainment.

As support of the round earth theory grew, exploration began. Moving through illusion, it was discovered that the earth was indeed round. The reality of a round earth opened

new areas of discussion and thought. As known knowledge changed, the entertainment changed. Theologians had to find another place for hell to exist. Artists had to find other subjects to paint. It was time to move forward.

Illusion And Reality Function Side By Side

Illusion and reality often function side by side. This sometimes makes it difficult to distinguish between the two.

Definition:

Illusion is the way you perceive things to be.

Reality is the way things really are. It may vary considerably from your perception of the way you think things are.

Most people, for example, intently project the positive part of themselves. They *try* to create the illusion that they only contain positive emotions, thoughts, words, and actions. They purposely suppress their negative side, *trying* to create an illusion for you—perhaps even for themselves. However, the reality is that people are dual-natured. They have positive and negative dimensions.

People work very hard to create illusions. Families create illusions that tell the outside world that they are happy and stable. The reality can be very different.

The advertising media takes great care to create illusions around their products so that you will buy them. Illusion tells

you that using a specific soap will make you happy, give you lots of energy, and bring fun and friends into your life. And this is only the beginning! Reality explains that using that specific soap only means that your physical body will be clean.

Illusion says that a soul in a fifty year-old body is wiser than one in a thirty year-old body. Realizing that people exist beyond the time frame of the body, reality may be completely different. The thirty year-old may be much further along in the evolutionary process.

Illusion tells people to eradicate crime. Reality explains that criminals are important. They provide the impetus for many people to grow. Because of them, law enforcement officers have the opportunity to learn many skills. These include defense, observation, concentration, teamwork, bravery, and compassion. Reality explains that criminals are equal in importance to law enforcement agencies.

Illusion tells people to eliminate disease. Yet doctors, nurses, pharmacies, drug companies, advertisers, researchers, and medical schools are a small sample of what would no longer be necessary without sick people. Reality explains that sick people are important to the health care profession.

Illusion Is Safe

Illusion is a safe place to be. You know who you are, how you act, how other people will act, and what your responses will be. Whether or not you like your life is inconsequential. What you have *right now* is the known. When you change, you move into the unknown. You have to think of new reactions to new people, activities, and situations. For this reason, it often feels safer to stay in illusion without searching for reality.

Reality brings with it a new perspective on old situations. The reality of a round earth opened up a new set of questions. Artists and theologians had to move out of the safe place that they had created for themselves. They had to create new answers to old situations. In a way, the rug was pulled out from underneath them.

In the same way, it sometimes seems easier to remain in your comfort zone. Moving into reality means finding parts of yourself from which you may be hiding. Finding these areas means looking, feeling, and dealing with them. It also means finding the freedom that comes with removing self-imposed limitations.

There is often a part of you that lives in the comfort of illusion. That part is not at all interested in changing. It enjoys the illusion. But it discourages you from moving through it to "reality". It tells you that illusion *is* reality. It works very hard to keep you there.

This part most likely contains many experiences that have never been completed or resolved. It tells you not to stir up painful memories that (you think) have been laid to rest long ago.

The reality, however, is that these memories live inside of you. Whether you are aware of it or not, you react to today through those memories. Sooner or later, in this lifetime or another, they must be resolved.

As an example, you might have felt unjustly punished as a child. At that time, it may not have been possible to express

those feelings. The child within still needs to be expressed. As an adult, you may think it is not appropriate to verbally express those feelings. As a release, making someone else feel bad does not really make you feel better.

To complete the experience, breathe yourself into your center. As an objective observer, allow it to rise to the surface. Allow the experience to pass before your inner eye. Observe the emotions that you feel. Allow the part of you that contains these emotions to yell, scream, cry, or do whatever it needs to do in order to cleanse itself.

Observe this part of yourself expressing to your Oversoul exactly how it feels. Ask your Oversoul to pass this message on to all other involved Oversouls. Ask that these Oversouls pass the message on to the involved individuals.

Releasing these buried memories may cause some discomfort. Old scars must sometimes be opened to promote inner healing. It takes a brave person to look at and experience those memories again. Realize that unresolved memories take up space within. Releasing them leaves room for peaceful feelings of inner harmony to grow.

Reality Explains

Illusion hides. Reality explains. A person who freely expresses anger toward you functions in an anger illusion. When you function in the same level of illusion, you express anger back. This contributes to the illusion that helps both of you understand anger.

Move through the illusion by being an objective observer and listener, instead of participating in it. Let reality explain that it is their own internal pain that causes them to be angry. Illusion tells that person to clean out the pain by giving it to others.

Reality explains that this is only a momentary buffer. Understanding the pain of this person allows you to have compassion for their inner struggles. You then no longer have to participate in this illusion because you understand beyond it. This moves you a layer closer to the reality of who you really are. Illusion entertains. However, there comes a point in all things when it is healthiest to move on.

Understand The Overall Plot

You did not create the play, but you are a part of the play. Illusion shows you only part of the script. Moving through illusion to reality is your real objective. This is vertical growth. Vertical growth allows you to see the play from above. From here, the overall plot is explained.

When you ask questions about reality, be sure that you pass them on up to your Oversoul and God. It is easy to get stuck in the space above your head that contains your own thoughts. Seeking answers from among your own thoughts limits those answers to the realm of known knowledge.

Reality explains that those answers must come from above, from your Oversoul and God. This allows your vision to open to new possibilities, moving you forward into "new" knowledge. Let the doors to the beyond open. Recognize that there are explanations that have not yet moved forward into your conscious mind, or perhaps into the entire collective conscious mind.

For instance, closing your mind to the possibility that criminals are a necessary part of the law enforcement play closes your mind to potential answers. Whenever you ask questions, be willing to hear the answers. Be willing to listen for answers that stretch you beyond current illusion and closer into reality. Your illusion of truth may be entirely different from the reality of truth.

Reality Expands And Grows

Reality expands and grows only as much as you let yourself grow. As you recognize and accept new ideas, reality explains that these concepts are ever-deep.

As an example, say you take up sculpting as a hobby. You learn the "how-to's" of sculpting that give it order. You accept the illusion that these rules cannot be broken or your project will fail. In effect, this illusion is your reality.

However, as you move deeper into the process you find that those rules can be broken, awakening the creativity within. You understand the basic set of rules and you recognize that you can go beyond them with satisfactory, or even better results. This moves you closer to reality. As with all things, the more time you devote to sculpting, the more the process continues to open up to you.

Initial illusion is important. It is a beginning point. Moving through it with understanding moves you into the next levels of learning. Reality expands and grows parallel to your own growth.

Knowledge changes illusion and reality. There will always be possibilities beyond what you now perceive. This is what keeps you interested and entertained. Finding new solutions is fascinating when you allow yourself to focus on the process. Move through and beyond illusion, allowing reality to explain, slowly, one step at a time, and always with an open mind.

EXPERIENCE IS NEUTRAL

All experience is neutral. Your reactions to experience label it "good" or "bad". Positive reactions label experience "good". Negative reactions label experience "bad". Reality explains that all experience is actually neutral, just as you are neutral and God is neutral. Consider some of the following examples:

* A small child is lost in the forest. He finds the forest intimidating and overwhelming. That child might describe the forest as dark, dreary, and lonely. Associating the forest with the feeling of being lost, he labels the forest "bad".

   On the other hand, as an adult he enjoys walking alone in the stillness of the forest. He associates the forest with feelings of peace and calm. Now, he labels the forest "good".

   But, is the forest itself really "good" or "bad"?

* A carpenter lives in an economically depressed area. Work is difficult to find. He associates his negative feelings about being a carpenter with lack of money. Eventually, he wonders if he has chosen the right pro-

fession. He labels the experience of being a carpenter "bad".

Ten years later the same geographic area is experiencing growth. There is plenty of work. The carpenter is financially secure. He associates his feelings about being a carpenter with success. Now, he labels the experience of being a carpenter "good".

But, is being a carpenter itself "good" or "bad"?

* A teen decides to learn how to ski. Once on the slopes, she realizes that she is afraid of heights. Skiing down the mountain gives her a runaway, panicky feeling. Associating the experience with those feelings, she labels skiing "bad".

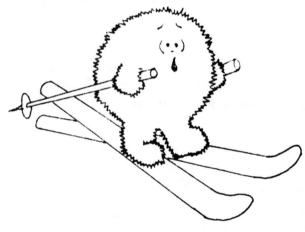

As she grows and matures, she learns to enjoy adventure. She loves the feeling of being outdoors and decides to try skiing again. Skiing down the mountain gives her a wonderful feeling of freedom. Now, she associates skiing with those feelings. She labels the experience "good".

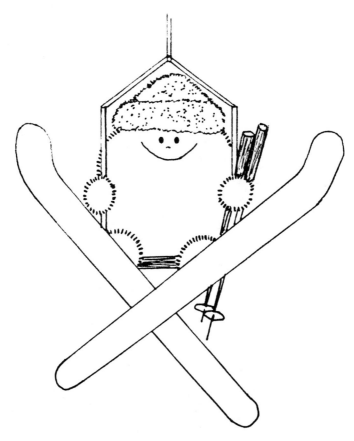

Is skiing itself "good" or "bad"?

Illusion says that positive and negative are separate. Reality explains that each explains one side of the same experience. When asked the question, "What is a forest?", the man in the first example can answer, "A forest is dark, dreary, and lonely. It can also be still, peaceful, and calm." Both the positive and negative reactions explain the reality of what a forest is. The forest itself remains neutral.

The carpenter can talk very knowledgeably about being a carpenter. He knows both the positives and negatives. Both explain about being a carpenter.

The woman who now enjoys skiing can explain to a novice what to expect the first time on skis. She understands the full scope of a single experience. The experience of skiing remains neutral.

Positive And Negative Labels

Choose to eliminate the word "bad" from your vocabulary. Many feelings are associated with the word "bad" that lead to judgment and criticism of self. Think in terms of "negative" qualities rather than "bad" qualities. Instead of labeling yourself "good" or "bad" merely acknowledge what does or does not exist within you.

There is nothing wrong with negative. Negative is part of the process. Put it in its proper perspective. Understand it for what it is.

Negative is not "bad". Negative promotes growth. It prevents stagnation, often prompting you to move forward. Rich with learning, it explains a part of God. *God is neither positive nor negative, but contains both.*

God provides all experience for you through your Oversoul. Give thanks for each one that comes your way. Learn from whatever is before you. Always remember that experience is neutral. It is your *reactions* that label experience either positive or negative.

Instead of quickly labeling an experience "negative", use some creative thinking. Circle around from the other side. Address it as a positive learning experience. As an objective observer, ask these questions:

What am I learning from this experience?

What weaknesses does it show me?

How can I eliminate my weaknesses?

What does it teach me about other people?

What does it teach me about life?

How will this experience make me a better or wiser person?

Your attitude changes when you take the time to answer these questions. Instead of fighting the experience, flow with it. You may even find yourself enjoying the challenge of the situation rather than avoiding it. Your entire perception changes. You start viewing difficult experiences as an opportunity for growth.

Positive is not better than negative. Each is equally necessary to understand the entire scope of a single experience. Throughout many lifetimes, you have experienced a variety of negatives. Now it is time to maintain your balance by experiencing the positives.

The Law Of Karma

There is a natural process of balance that maintains your identity as neutral energy. This is the Law of Karma. In other words, every negative experience is balanced with a positive one. This maintains your neutral state. This can be described as follows:

$$(-1) \qquad + \qquad (+1) \qquad = \qquad 0$$

Negative Experience + Positive Experience = Neutrality

For every negative (-1) that is added to your list of experiences, a positive (+1) is added so that you always equal neutrality (0). The examples given in the beginning of the chapter showed balance being achieved very quickly in this lifetime. However, because you exist for eons, you may take many lifetimes to attain balance.

Consider this. You have an unstable marriage (-1) in this lifetime. The Law of Karma applied says that eventually you will experience a stable marriage (+1). Your experiences teach you what marriage is (+1) and what marriage is not (-1). The experience of marriage itself remains neutral.

Sometimes people literally interpret the Law of Karma as "an eye for an eye, a tooth for a tooth". But the Law of Karma goes beyond that. It exists to help people understand the full spectrum of their experiences.

For instance, at some point in your life you may have *given* (+1) selflessly of yourself. At a later time when you needed help, someone was there to give it to you. You *took* (-1) help. Giving and taking helps explain the full spectrum of one experience. Move through the illusion that negative is "bad". Negative is just negative.

Karmic Bonds

The Law of Karma maintains bonds between one or more people. With agreement on the inner levels, these bonds allow each participant to understand the full spectrum of a single experience. Allan asks his friend Joe out to play. He shows

Joe a wonderful tree that he has just discovered. In his enthusiasm, Joe eagerly climbs the tree. He falls, breaking a leg. This could not have happened without Joe's approval on the inner levels. At some point, he asked the question:

"What are legs?"

Two healthy legs explain legs. They answer the questions:

What is it like to have legs? What can I do with them? (Having legs explains legs.)

A broken leg limits one's activities. The questions become:

What might it be like not to have legs? What can I do without them? (Not having legs explains legs.)

In other words, having legs and not having legs both answer the same question.

Allan chose to play the role that helped Joe answer his question. At some point in time, they may choose to reverse the roles. They both agree to maintain this karmic bond.

Examples Of Karmic Bonds

Karmic bonds exist among all life forms. You may have hurt an animal in one lifetime. In the next, that animal might be your treasured pet. Both experiences teach you about animals.

In one lifetime, you may choose an occupation that destroys the environment. In another, you may choose to find the solution to prevent damage you caused. Both lifetimes teach you about the environment.

Perhaps you had a lifetime where you had great respect for the earth. You gave (+1) respect. In this lifetime you are a prosperous farmer. You take (-1) the fruits of the earth. This experience also teaches you about the environment.

You may have had a lifetime where you were very poor, yet you shared (+1) whatever you had with whomever needed it. Perhaps in this lifetime you win the lottery. Those whom you helped, put their money into a system that in turn distributes it to you. You now take (-1) from others. This teaches you about prosperity.

Again, keep in mind that negative is not "bad". Negative is just one side of a single experience. Always remember that the Law of Karma exists for you.

Question Your Oversoul

Understanding that experience is neutral puts all experience in perspective. On some level of awareness you invite all experience into your life, even ones that are very painful. All experience teaches you.

Whenever you have an experience that you do not understand, question your Oversoul as an objective observer and listener. Ask for help to move through the illusion of "good" and "bad" into the reality that explains. You may get satis-factory answers to some questions. To others, you may get only partial answers. File partial answers away. Like the crossword puzzle, one day those partial answers will have meaning.

All experience promotes growth. Find out why you asked for a particular experience. Establish the learning that it brought. Then ask your Oversoul to build on that learning, taking you deeper inside of yourself.

ORGANIZE YOUR ENERGY

With so many activities to choose from, it is important to organize your personal (psychic) energy. Organizing it in conscious awareness allows you to use it efficiently. Efficient use of psychic energy allows you to increase the number of vertical experiences in each day.

Because you operate within the constraints of a twenty-four hour time period, your day only accommodates a given number of activities. A specified amount of time every day must be devoted to constants. Eating, sleeping, dressing, and personal hygiene are examples of constants. They cannot be eliminatcd, but you may be able to perform them more efficiently.

Evaluate Simple Tasks

Evaluate some of the simple tasks that you perform every day. Determine if they could be accomplished in a more efficient way. This does not mean rushing through tasks. Rather, it means performing the same task while expending less time, energy, and effort.

When preparing meals, for example, stop and think before you act. As an objective observer, evaluate the task. The following are samples of questions you might ask:

Do I need to make five trips to the refrigerator?

or

Could I accomplish the same thing in two trips?

Do I need to go into the pantry four times for four different ingredients?

or

Could I get everything in one trip?

Do I need to make one trip to the cupboard for dishes, one trip to a drawer for silverware, and one trip to another drawer for napkins?

or

Could I get everything out at once while standing in the same place?

Without rushing, you prepare the meal in a much more efficient way. You spend less psychic energy by taking the time to stop and think before you act. Every bit of energy saved gives you time and energy to spend elsewhere.

Saving energy throughout the day extends the twenty-four hour time period. Performing the same number of tasks in a more efficient way gives you "extra" time to add other experiences to the day. It might be walking, reading, relaxing, or completing unfinished projects. What activities would you add if you had "extra" time?

Most likely, thinking before you act will help you perform many daily tasks more efficiently while expending less energy. This continues to develop the creative thinking process. You perform very ordinary tasks in extraordinary ways.

Body Tension Requires Energy

Think how much energy it takes to hold tension in the body. To illustrate this point, make a fist with your right hand. Squeeze it as hard as you can for sixty seconds. Your hand represents the tension that you hold in the body. After sixty seconds your hand is tired. You expend psychic energy to maintain tension. Releasing tension from the body adds to your pool of "extra" energy.

With your thoughts, feel and evaluate where you hold tension in the body. Squeeze your hand again to remember how tension feels. Now relax it so you know how relaxation feels. Release those feelings to your Oversoul.

Get in touch with every part of your body. Feel and release all tension. Begin at your feet, and slowly move up the lower legs, knees, upper legs, buttocks, lower back, middle back, upper back, shoulders, neck, head, upper arms, elbows, lower arms, and hands. When you find parts that hold tension, release that tension up to your Oversoul. Then relax that part. Make an effort to feel those parts a few times a day. Determine if they are in a state of tension or relaxation. Each time you release tension, you add to your "extra" energy pool. That "extra" energy can be used for something constructive.

Think Before You Speak Or Act

Stop and think before you speak or act. Every time you choose to expend negative energy, you make the decision to give up positive energy. When you express hate, you consciously decide to give up love. If you give out anxiety, you give up peace and calm. If you give out harshness, you give up softness.

Whatever you give out always returns from whence it comes. Negative energy going out means negative energy coming back. Hate going out means hate coming back. Anxiety brings back anxiety. Harshness means harshness coming back. Be aware of the consequences of the actions you choose.

Assume responsibility for your actions. Make conscious decisions of what and how you want to express. As an objective observer:

Observe yourself choose what and how you will express.

Observe yourself act out that expression.

Observe the effect of your actions on yourself, your environment, and others.

Act in conscious awareness. Be aware of both the positive and negative consequences of your actions at any given moment. When you choose to expend negative energy, observe yourself. As the objective observer, ask these questions:

How does this make
me feel?

How does this make
my body feel?

How does this make
other people feel?

How does this affect my
environment?

Do I really want to act
this way?

Am I ready to release
this part, or some of
this part, to my Oversoul?

Release all observations up to your Oversoul. Acknowledge responsibility for your actions. Also acknowledge your willingness to assume the consequences of those actions. Always keep in mind that consciously choosing to expend negative energy means giving up positive energy somewhere in your life.

Giving Energy To Others

On some level of awareness, you may choose to give your energy to others. This happens in a variety of ways. You may be giving physical, mental, emotional, spiritual, or even monetary support to someone who needs to be doing these things for him/herself. Very often, people willingly hand over their responsibilities when given the choice.

You may be the easy way out for them to solve their challenges. Be a catalyst by giving them tools. But always remember, they need the satisfaction of solving their own challenges. They need the learning and growth that their challenges bring them. Always determine through the involved Oversouls who you need to help and how.

Choose Vertical Growth Activities

You always have many activities to choose from. Do your best to choose the ones that promote vertical growth. Eliminate the ones that promote horizontal growth. You may belong to basketball, volleyball, and baseball teams. Are all three important? Maybe they are and maybe they are not. This is a choice only you can determine.

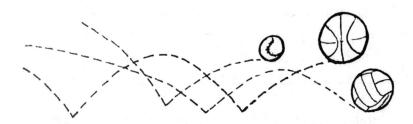

All activities are merely tools that teach you about yourself. Evaluate your activity by asking some of the following questions:

Does it—

lighten my life?

help me learn to change?

develop my creative thinking process?

promote positive or negative growth?

teach me something that no other activity provides?

pull me up into my potential, keep me where I am, or pull me down?

Ask questions that are specific to your individual growth. Consciously decide what you want in your life and why. Giving up activities that you no longer need allows doors to open for new activities that match your current level of development.

Spend Meditation Time Wisely

Choose to spend your meditation time wisely. There is only a certain length of time available to devote to this level of deep inner concentration. Devote that time to accessing information that you need *right now.*

There will always be many questions that you *could* ask your Oversoul, such as:

How can I read auras?

How can I have an out-of-body experience?

What is my future?

What are all of my past lifetimes?

How did the universe begin?

However, for now build your foundation. Concentrate on questions that specifically create inner harmony at this moment. Use the following questions as a guideline:

How can I change so my days flow smoother?

How can I improve my relationships?

What parts of myself am I ready to let go?

How can I bring order into my life?

How can I communicate with others more effectively?

How can I move deeper into my center?

Taking the time to do this daily ritual brings you into balance in a slow, methodical way. As that balance is achieved, the answers to the other questions will surface naturally.

Ask For Wisdom With Knowledge

Whenever you ask for knowledge, always ask for the wisdom to use it correctly. A child asking for power tools to create beautiful woodwork is asking for something beyond his skill level. He does not yet understand the accompanying responsibilities. Those potentially wonderful tools can do extensive damage without the wisdom to use them correctly. The child may seriously injure himself. Only after he hurts himself will he fully understand the consequences and his inability to use them properly. That may be of little comfort.

Like that child, your current scope of knowledge is limited. Whenever you ask for anything, *always* state that you only want whatever is in your best interest. Knowledge that you are not ready for may do more damage than good.

Do not wait until after the fact to understand why you were not given access to particular knowledge. Accept the wisdom of your Oversoul. Ask for knowledge that is pertinent to your immediate growth. Become strong and versatile in the present moment. When deeper truths are revealed to you, let it be through the natural process of unfoldment. Your Oversoul will always show you what you *need* to know. It is your responsibility to be open and receptive to the information. What you *want* to know and what you *need* to know can be very different. Trust your Oversoul to know what is best.

Making Specific Choices

Organizing your energy allows you to make specific choices quickly for very mundane activities. Shopping is a wonderful way to learn how efficient you can become. For instance, why do you have to handle several heads of lettuce before you choose the "right" one? Why not ask your Oversoul to direct you to "your" head the first time?

A remodeling project may call for specific tools. Ask your Oversoul to direct you to the store with the best price on the item you need. Why do you need to go into several stores for the tools when one will do?

Need an attorney? Look in the phone book. Ask your Oversoul to direct you to the best one for you. Allow yourself to find the most suitable person for the job the first time. Apply the same principle to all your activities. Apply it when you meet a new client, go on vacation, or clean your closets. All of this efficiency allows you to add to that "extra" energy pool that you are in the process of creating.

Use Universal Energy

Organized energy increases your awareness of the universal energy that flows up and down. Every time you stop and think before you act or speak, you send your thoughts up to your Oversoul. Then you wait for a feeling to come back down to you. Each time you move your psychic energy up instead of out, you allow your Oversoul to cleanse it and send it back to you on a new level of awareness.

By doing this, you apply very basic metaphysical laws to very basic activities. You are not doing anything extraordinary, you simply are using the laws. All it takes is a willingness to begin in the beginning and *try.*

Start with simple tasks. Associate feelings of success with those simple tasks. Then work your way up to more complex activities. Learn the basics first. Realize that it takes time to build your foundation.

You are faced with dozens of ways to spend your energy every day. How you choose to organize and spend it is always your option. For example:

You can—

perform your daily tasks efficiently or inefficiently.

maintain tension in your body or release it.

give your energy away or keep it.

express positive or negative energy.

ask questions out of curiosity or need during meditation.

work with your Oversoul or without it.

Whatever you decide to do, do so in awareness. Think before you speak or act, taking the time to evaluate the potential results of your decisions.

Organizing your energy allows you to make room for more vertical experiences. This means more learning, growth, and eventually more inner knowledge and harmony.

DURING THE PROCESS

The tools and principles you are learning automatically move you into a deeper awareness of all that is real. The tools move you forward into your potential, giving guidance along the way. During the process, they instigate new inner activity.

This stirs up buried experiences, feelings, habit responses, vibratory imprints, knowledge, and lifetimes. Because this changes the status quo, you move into unfamiliar territory. As with any change, you may feel uncomfortable at first. But as you move deeper, you also must move through these feelings of discomfort.

On one day, you feel very good about moving in a new direction. The next, you feel depressed because you realize how much of yourself is being released. You may even feel empty when you release old habit responses and vibratory imprints that have been important to you for lifetimes. You actually move into a type of death experience when you part with something that was very meaningful. As with any death, it takes time to adjust. Feel compassion for yourself as you move through the loss. Remember, you may always maintain contact with old parts of yourself through your Oversoul.

Whenever you feel empty inside, ask your Oversoul to fill up the empty spaces with:

Pink energy for love.

or

Blue energy for peace and calm.

or

Green energy for healing.

Release all that you feel up to your Oversoul.

Reality explains that all these feelings exist to move you into the final stage of the releasing process. Old vibratory imprints *try* to pull you back. New vibratory imprints grow stronger, *trying* to pull you into them. At this point, you finally release old habit responses and vibratory imprints. You automatically move into the *being* stage.

When you *try* very hard to move forward, you may even feel like you are standing still. You may feel restless because you are unable to detect inner growth. As long as you *try,* be assured that something, somewhere is being stirred around.

Progress In A Methodical Manner

These tools and principles help you progress in a methodical, balanced manner. It may not always be easy to identify specific growth.

As a child, you were not consciously aware when your physical body grew. Yet, it still grew. One arm did not suddenly become six inches longer than the other. One foot did not suddenly require a much larger shoe than the other foot. Every part of your physical body grew in direct proportion to every other part.

In the same way, you progress in a methodical, balanced manner on many levels of awareness. Your conscious, subconscious, and superconscious minds all work together to maintain a state of inner balance. These minds often work at the same time on different subjects.

As further explanation, think about a time when you were driving. Suddenly, you arrive at your destination. You realize that you were daydreaming, and cannot actually remember driving the car. What part of your mind drove the car without getting you killed? What part of your mind was off wandering? Two parts of your mind functioned at the same time, each on different subjects, each on different levels. As you continue to bring more knowledge forward into your conscious mind, you become aware of the three minds working together.

Bring The Body Into Balance

The body is only a home for the real you. But, it is vital that it receive proper care to allow you to reach optimum mental and spiritual levels. This is necessary for you to express new knowledge. Therefore, as your mental and spiritual food changes, the physical food you give your body must also change. This allows the body to continue balancing itself with the mind and spirit.

The food your body craves may automatically change as you change. The food that you put into the body is symbolic of the food that you put into your mind. By listening to the body, you can help it make the necessary adjustments in conscious awareness.

When the body is hungry, ask it what it *needs*. Then use the listening skills that you are acquiring, and pay attention. Separate the *wants* of the taste buds from the *needs* of the body. It is possible to satisfy the *wants* of the taste buds, without satisfying the *needs* of the body.

The stomach and intestinal tract can be full while the body itself is hungry for specific nutrients. This means that you continually put more food into it than it needs, while it *tries* to extract nutrients that just are not there. The end result is extra unwanted weight.

Pay attention to how it feels after eating various foods. Feel what makes it strong and healthy, and what makes it weak. Listening through your Oversoul, communicate with it by asking specific questions. Ask it if it wants:

Protein—
  Red meat, meat, seafood, nuts, dairy products.

Vegetables—
  Green, yellow; cooked, raw.

Fruits—
  Citrus, bananas, apples; cooked, raw.

Grain—
  Wheat, oats, barley, millet; bread; crackers; cooked or cold.

Dairy products—
  Milk, cheese, yogurt.

As you eat, ask the body to tell you when it has had enough. The *taste buds* may want more food, but the *body* may have had an adequate amount.

Sometimes, the body may require foods that you think are unhealthy for it. White sugar, for example, may irritate the nerves, but for some people it helps to ground them. If this is the case, determine how much white sugar is *needed*, not *wanted*, and stop there. Salt may irritate the blood veins, but it also cuts mucus in the body. Pay attention to what the body needs, for whatever reason.

Changing your diet too quickly may throw the body into a "healing crisis". Simply put, it can become sick. Just as a drug addict suffers withdrawal symptoms, the body may suffer withdrawal symptoms from certain types of foods, specifically:

White sugar.

White flour.

Salt.

Flesh foods.

Processed foods.

Alcohol.

Chemicals and preservatives.

Any time you decide to change your diet, take a few minutes to explain the new plan to your body. Ask its cooperation, and thank it for its help.

Eliminate unnecessary foods from your diet by gradually reducing the intake. This puts less stress on the body, decreasing the possibility of a "healing crisis". Sometimes, you may get sick anyway. This only means that old toxins from unnecessary vibratory imprints are on their way out of the body. Instead of becoming discouraged, merely send them on their way up to your Oversoul. Thank them for the learning that they brought you. Continue to ask the body to teach you how to strengthen it. If you take the time to listen, it will instruct you.

Moving Through The Layers

The tools that you are acquiring move you through many layers of experience. Each layer contains a part of the one on top of it. For instance, each one contains some resentment, fear, guilt, low self-esteem, as well as some contentment, courage, harmony, or high self-esteem.

As you move through one layer, you feel good because you think that you have released all of your resentment. Then when you least expect it, resentment shows up again. You wonder where it came from. You thought you had released it from your life.

You merely touch into the next layer. Then you move through resentment again. Finally, when you think that it is gone, it shows up again. Because you are tired of moving through resentment, this may disappoint you.

You like the thrill of learning new principles, applying them, and having immediate results. Now you have to dig a little deeper. You may have to wait a little longer for results. This is because you are moving into deeper areas of yourself.

Cleaning

When you feel really stuck, cleaning is a simple activity that may get you moving again. Discarding old, unnecessary possessions is symbolic of discarding old, unnecessary habit responses and vibratory imprints. The outer always reflects the inner. This is a law. An outer change anywhere automatically changes something inside.

You do not have to start a major cleaning campaign. Clean out your briefcase, a drawer in your desk, a shelf in your closet. Pull a few weeds, rake a few leaves, plant a few flowers. Paint or redecorate. Wash a window or two. Dispose of anything that you no longer need or appreciate. Any cleaning, anywhere will prompt change.

Walking

Walking also helps move you. Walking brings the physical body into balance. When one shifts, they all must shift because body, mind, and spirit are interconnected. This, too, is a law. Balancing the body helps create the shift that brings *you* into balance.

As you walk, hang your arms at your side. Allow them to swing freely, without burdening them with packages or purses. Be aware of the shift in body weight from left to right, and right to left. You may walk many miles before the corresponding mental and spiritual shifts occur. When these shifts occur, new avenues of action will become apparent.

Sleeping

Sleeping patterns sometimes change during the process of inner growth. You may suddenly need more or less sleep. Buried turbulence may rise up into your conscious mind during the night, resulting in nightmares and/or bad dreams. Review and release these dreams up to your Oversoul.

Holding Patterns

Your growth may move into a holding pattern while waiting for other players to move into their places. Others also have lessons that they must complete. They develop the skills that they need in order to move into your life. When everyone is ready, the next act will begin.

Ask Your Oversoul Questions

Whenever you want to move but are not sure how, remember to ask your Oversoul questions. Your Oversoul is dependent on you for feedback. You are now a partner in the growth process. Your questions help your Oversoul determine your strengths and weaknesses, and how to correctly move you.

Learn to interpret the responses that your Oversoul gives you. Sometimes it is difficult to feel the response of your Oversoul. It is easy to stop in the space above your head that contains your own thoughts. Remember to push your thoughts up high until you connect with your Oversoul. Eventually, you will recognize that there is a specific feeling when you have made the connection.

Remember, you are in the process of learning Oversoul communication. You do not have perfect Oversoul communication yet. Compare yourself to children learning to walk. Only practice will teach them to walk. Eventually the children *will* walk.

Moving Incorrectly

Rather than move incorrectly, you may make a conscious decision to do nothing at all. Fear and ego may tell you to stand still, rather than risk making a mistake. Moving incorrectly for any situation is not "wrong". It merely indicates to your Oversoul where you need guidance.

Your Oversoul then helps you bring that part of yourself into balance. The first step in change is to *try*. As long as you *try*, you will be given direction.

If you choose to stand still, your Oversoul will *try* to get you to move. This may be in the form of a negative learning experience because you know how to react to the negative. This gives you a chance to move, even though it is through your "old" learning process.

If you continue to ignore the negative learning experience, you will stagnate. Your Oversoul then has the option of removing you from the physical body. It can choose to place you into a new situation, where you have no choice but to move. When in doubt, always remember:

It is better to move incorrectly than not to move at all.

Keep Moving Forward

Recognizing the progress that you have made toward inner awareness is wonderful. You acknowledge where you were and where you are now. Sometimes you become so appreciative of your growth that you reach a plateau. The present looks so good in comparison to the past that you let illusion tell you that life cannot get any better. So you decide to stop growing.

When you believe illusion, you let go of the momentum that keeps you moving forward. Always remember that behind unopened doors are experiences and knowledge waiting for you to enter. Reality explains that your growth is still in progress. Enjoy and appreciate where you are. But allow your past to be part of the motivating force that continues to propel you into your potential.

Appreciate The Present

As doors begin to open, you start to realize your potential. This may make you dissatisfied and impatient with the present. You may even allow bitterness to creep in as you wish to be "there" instead of "here".

Completion of current lessons is necessary in order to be strong enough to claim your potential when the time is right. Illusion tells you that you want to be the finished product. Reality explains that there is no finished product. You just keep growing. You are infinitely deep. Your journey is forever.

You are here to enjoy each period of transition—

From the beginning...

through the middle...

onto the end.

Then you go on to the next experience, and the next, and the next. You only exist for experience.

BLENDING IT ALL TOGETHER

Once there was a businessman who had a successful business, a beautiful family, and a supportive network of friends. Yet, he still felt an emptiness inside. He longed to know more about God and the mysteries of life. His constant prayer to God was, "Teach me about you. Teach me about who and what you are."

One day while meditating he was shown a lifetime during which he was a monk living in a monastery. He lived a cloistered life and had ample time for contemplation and meditation. His constant prayer to God was, "Teach me about you. Teach me about who and what you are."

In that lifetime God answered him and said, "I will teach you about me. I will teach you about who and what I am. I will give you a lifetime with a successful business, a beautiful family, and a supportive network of friends. This will help to explain who and what I am."

All that is comes out of God.

Illusion tells you that God is separate from the outer material world. Reality explains that it is all the same. The division of spiritual versus non-spiritual functions is only an illusion of human thought.

This world is created by God. All that exists is a part of God. All that exists has a purpose. When you do not understand that purpose, you may label a certain activity "non-spiritual" or even "bad".

In effect, this is a judgment and criticism of God's world. With your Oversoul and God, you created the very small role that you play. However, only God created the overall drama. As you release the need to judge self, the need to judge the outer world decreases. Remember, the outer always reflects the inner and vice versa.

Just as with self, learn to accept what is. As an objective observer ask your Oversoul and God to *explain* the purpose of what exists. Send your questions up through your own thoughts to your Oversoul. Wait for the answers to come back down the channel. If you do not receive any explanation, continue to send your questions up. When you are ready the answers will come back down.

Instead of *trying* to invoke *your* will upon creation, allow creation to be. This acceptance and understanding automatically moves you vertically. From this new position, you see the big picture more clearly.

As an example, remember that there are Oversouls for all of creation. There are Oversouls for the mineral, plant, and animal kingdoms, as well as humankind. Each kingdom is in the process of experiencing God. So in turn, a car is merely

120

part of the mineral kingdom in the process of experiencing. It answers many questions for God about what the mineral kingdom is and is not.

Illusion says that you own the car. Reality explains that you are only together through mutual agreement. When the car is through with you, it will be sold, wrecked, or fall apart.

Cars help answer the question, "What is the mineral kingdom?". Cars have an important part in the play. They challenge humankind to bring untapped knowledge forward into the collective conscious mind. That knowledge is needed to move into the next level of transportation. As a part of God, cars deserve respect.

All that exists deserves respect for the part that it plays in the overall drama. Respect for self is reflected by respect for the outer world. Consider some of the following areas that illusion labels "non-spiritual".

Money

Illusion often labels money "non-spiritual". Reality explains that money is as spiritual as prayer and meditation. They both originate from God. Money is a neutral medium of exchange that allows experience. It represents expended energy.

A ship builder exchanges the intangible energy spent building a ship for a tangible representation of that energy. That tangible representation is called "money". It represents the expended energy. Money creates a balancing cycle—energy going out, energy coming in.

The exchange of money for goods and services continues the balancing cycle. Someone expends intangible energy to create goods and services. In turn, he/she is given a tangible representation.

Money also simplifies. Without money, the world would operate entirely on a barter system. In many instances that is acceptable. But what if you are a dentist? You may want some apples from the orchardist down the road. He may not need any dental work in exchange. In a moneyless system even a simple task such as getting apples may become complex.

Redefining money puts it into its proper perspective. The outer world always reflects the inner world. Money is symbolic of energy. Not having enough money to meet your *needs* is a form of self-denial. In a way this says, "I am not worthy of receiving the equivalent of my energy expenditure". If this is the case, use the following affirmations as new seed thoughts:

I release the need for lack.

I am worthy of money.

I accept money as a part of God's world.

I deserve to experience God's abundant supply of energy.

Accepting money into your life acknowledges that God provides enough energy for you to comfortably, and simply, experience the outer world.

Your Body

Illusion often labels your body "non-spiritual". Reality explains that your body is part of the process. You are not the body, but you operate in and through it. It is an instrument that is refined daily with thoughts and actions as well as diet and exercise. Fine-tuning the instrument that is provided for you ensures efficient communication between yourself, your Oversoul, and God.

Anytime that you judge or criticize your body, you dissipate the psychic energy that maintains it. This accelerates physical aging and deterioration. Instead, evaluate your body. Set a goal to improve it.

Just because your body is not sick does not mean that it is healthy. Ask for guidance to create health within it through thought, actions, diet, and exercise. Ask it what it needs to maintain its health.

Communicate with it. When you listen to it you may be surprised at what you learn. Offer it to your Oversoul and God. Ask that it be blessed and loved. Use the following affirmations as new seed thoughts:

I release the need to judge and criticize my body.

I love and appreciate my body.

I listen to my body and allow it to teach me.

I ask my Oversoul and God to bless and love my body.

Go beyond accepting your body. Take the time to love and appreciate it. Thank it for working with you.

Play And Rest

Illusion often says that play and rest are "non-spiritual" activities. Reality explains that play and rest create balance. Together they help you:

Break up patterns that are too serious and intense.

Lighten your attitudes.

Become more flexible.

Develop distance from your everyday routine.

View life as an objective observer.

Quiet and calm your conscious mind.

Replenish the psychic energy of your body.

Above all, play and rest allow the mind and body to *relax.* Tension causes blood veins to constrict. This decreases the flow of blood carrying essential oxygen to the brain and other vital organs. As a result, the mind and body function less efficiently. Spiritual growth slows when the necessary instrument (your body) does not function at optimum capacity.

In a relaxed state, blood flows more freely throughout the body. Psychic energy circulates through the body with less restraints. Efficient functioning of the physical body increases mental capacity. In response, spiritual growth accelerates.

When you "let go, you let God", as the saying goes. Play and rest help you let go. In a relaxed state, inner communication is able to come forward into your conscious mind. How many times have you struggled at length through an activity with unsuccessful results? Usually, the answer comes to you not long after you give up and walk away. You finally "let go".

Play and rest are productive activities that are essential to physical, mental, and spiritual growth. Use the following affirmations as new seed thoughts:

I deserve to play and rest.

I deserve balance in my life.

I allow myself to relax.

I "let go and let God."

Everything that is produced in the outer world has its origin in the inner world. Play and rest help to establish the pathway that takes you within.

Occupation

Illusion may label your occupation as a "non-spiritual" activity. Reality explains that all activity is spiritual. Everything that you do, you do for God. If you are a minister, the outer world labels your occupation "spiritual". If you work on an assembly line, it is up to *you* to label your occupation "spiritual". In other words, this gives *you* the responsibility to identify yourself. Your identity now comes from within instead of from the outer world.

Occupations always reflect the present. Your occupation will teach you if you let it. Your occupation may allow you to expend physical energy to drain inner anger. Your occupation may help you to move through fear. Or, it may keep you in fear. Service occupations may allow you to balance past actions through present activities—if, in the past you "took" (-1), now you are "giving" (+1).

Occupations are also an acknowledgment of acquired skills in this lifetime and others. Lifetimes travel in cycles. Your occupation is a key that tells you who you were and what experiences brought you to this point in time.

To better understand your occupation, use the following affirmations as new seed thoughts:

I recognize that all activity is spiritual.

I offer my work to my Oversoul and God.

I allow my occupation to teach me about my present.

I allow my occupation to teach me about my past.

Your occupation provides a wonderful opportunity for you to blend inner and outer activity.

Redefine Life

Redefine any part of life that you criticize or judge because it is "non-spiritual". Remember that any outer criticism or judgment is only a reflection of inner criticism or judgment. As you accept self as is, you accept the outer world as is.

Acceptance of self leads to respect for the part of God that you are. In turn, you respect the outer world for the part of

God that it is. Continue to evaluate all activity, releasing to your Oversoul what you no longer need. Then move forward into the next experience, always remembering that—

Everything is equal in importance.

Everything is spiritual.

Everything exists for God.

SPIRITUALITY SURROUNDS YOU

Spirituality is a moment-by-moment daily occurrence. Every moment is a function of God. Each one is equally meaningful. One is not more or less spiritual than another. Illusion may tell you to go out in search of spirituality. Reality explains that all you have to do is remain in your center and accept what is already yours. Spirituality is a state of inner being.

Each moment in your life reflects your state of inner being. Whatever you choose to put in your moments defines your personal spirituality. How you treat yourself, others, and the outer world reflects your state of inner being.

Spirituality is private and personal. You do not need to tell or show others how spiritual you are. The more that you accomplish on the inner levels, the cleaner and clearer you stay. You teach others simply by *being*. On some level of awareness they notice that your body, mind, and spirit express something "different":

Your body is relaxed.

Your words are clear.

Your surrounding space is clean.

You listen and observe objectively.

Your energy moves up and down instead of back and forth.

Your energy is gathered in one place and is strong and solid.

You have respect for self, others, and the outer world.

You are noticed just because. There is no ego involved, or any outer expression of inner devotion. You just are.

Spirituality Is Comfortable

As you discover and define your own inner state of being, you find that spirituality encompasses your life in a very natural, comfortable way. Your inner world easily integrates with the outer world. You find that all your activities easily meld into a single expression of spirituality.

This process acknowledges what already exists. The difference is that you now allow everything to be a part of you. Illusion taught you to separate. Reality explains that everything is one and the same. Everything answers the questions:

Who am I?

What am I?

Who is God?

What is God?

Spirituality surrounds you. It has always been there. It will always be there. Acknowledge and accept what is already yours.

THE KNOWLEDGE IS YOURS

Everything takes practice, including moving deeper inside of yourself. The knowledge is fascinating, the process endless. Each time you establish and understand one set of knowledge, the next set automatically unveils itself.

What was once mysterious and secretive is now simple and explicable. It has order and meaning. Knowledge that explains the inner world also explains the outer, and vice versa. It is rewarding to see your own life simplify as a result of applying that knowledge.

Practice, Practice, Practice!

The knowledge is in place waiting for you to "discover" it. The next step is yours. The speed and depth of your personal growth is up to you.

Are you willing to:

keep an open mind?

let go of the old?

look at yourself with honesty?

try new methods and techniques?

practice, practice, practice?

Anyone who is an expert on anything has undoubtedly spent numerous hours studying the subject. That is how one becomes an expert: ask questions, test theories, and practice, practice, practice!

New techniques and methods in any field require practice. Personal growth is no different. The degree of expertise you develop is dependent upon the time and intensity that you wish to devote to yourself. How important are you to yourself?

Understand Your Own Microcosmic Mystery

This second book has established growth possibilities, along with tools and techniques for taking yourself there. With time and practice, understand your own microcosmic mystery by:

establishing vertical growth as a goal.

observing and listening objectively.

learning how to change.

identifying and releasing old, unnecessary habit responses.

moving through illusion into reality.

understanding the neutrality of experience.

organizing your psychic energy.

taking care of body, mind, and spirit.

respecting yourself and the outer world.

Each subject area listed above probably has more answers than you have questions. This means that each is ripe for exploration. Decide for yourself how deep you want to explore and the time you want to devote. But whatever your decision, make it in conscious awareness.

Your Path Is In Place

As you leave behind old behavior patterns and ways of thinking, appreciate the experiences and lessons that they brought. Continue moving forward on your path as it becomes clearer and more accessible . Your path is in place, waiting to be utilized. You already stand upon it. Feel the freedom that comes from "Moving Forward"!

Blessings,

Janet Dian

APPENDICES

SOME THINGS TO TRY

OBSERVE

Observe your body language.

At what point in conversations does it change?

Does your body express itself differently with different people?

* * *

Observe the colors that you choose to wear.

Do you wear some colors more than others?

Does one color make you feel different than another color?

Do you choose specific colors for specific occasions?

* * *

Observe the people that you choose to have around you.

What do they teach you about yourself?

What specific reactions do specific people bring out in you?

LISTEN

Listen to your words.

> Do they affirm the positive or negative in your life?

*　*　*

Listen to the tone of your voice.

> Do you like what you hear?

*　*　*

Listen to the feelings behind your words.

> Do your words match your feelings?

*　*　*

Listen to the energy behind your words.

> Do you like the feeling of the energy?

*　*　*

Listen to the colors that you use when you speak.

> What do they tell you about yourself?

*　*　*

When you are very quiet, listen to the vibrations around yourself.

> What secrets do they share about your state of inner being?

RELEASE JUDGMENT AND CRITICISM OF SELF

Choose to replace the word "bad" with the word "negative".

As you observe and evaluate inner qualities, think in terms of "positive" and "negative".

Observe your feelings to determine if this makes you feel less judgmental and critical of yourself.

CHANGE

Do three ordinary tasks in an extraordinary way. Decide if you want to do this for a day, a week, or even a month. Write these down. Then observe how you feel.

Did you successfully accomplish these small changes?

Did you feel enjoyment or stress?

If you felt awkward, was it okay that you felt awkward?

Did these small changes help open the creative thinking process?

Is change easy, difficult, or somewhere in between for you?

Does making these small changes affect your ability to implement larger, more significant change?

HABIT RESPONSES

What situations and/or people always evoke the same reactions from you?

Do you like these reactions?

If not, how would you like to respond?

Resolve to stop and think before you act the next time.

Give yourself credit even if you stop and think after the fact.

Acknowledge any progress you make, regardless of how insignificant it may seem.

SPEND YOURSELF WISELY

Choose three simple tasks.

Determine how to perform them more efficiently.

Try the new way.

Evaluate your feelings.

Does performing them more efficiently add to your energy pool?

How would you use "extra" energy if you had it?

Are there other tasks that might be performed more efficiently?

CLEAN YOUR HOME

Choose something in your home or workplace that needs cleaning. Set a goal that is obtainable even if it is one drawer or half of a closet. After you have cleaned it, observe how you feel.

Does it make you feel good to get it in order?

Did getting rid of unnecessary items make your mental house feel lighter or emptier, or both?

Do you somehow feel cleaned out?

WHAT DO YOU LIKE ABOUT YOURSELF?

Make a list of ten qualities or traits that you like about yourself.

Is this easy or difficult?

Always take time to appreciate who you are and what you have accomplished.

AFFIRMATIONS

AFFIRMATIONS

Choose one or two of the following affirmations. Make any changes that personalize them for you. Think, say, or write them throughout your day. The more you utilize them, the faster they will move you.

BALANCING THE BODY

I release the need for excess weight.

I release the need for food that is unhealthy for my body.

I deserve to have a healthy body.

I listen to my body.

I release the need for body tension.

My body is relaxed and at peace.

I easily separate the needs from the wants of my body.

CENTERING

I breathe myself into my center.

My center is strong and flexible.

I remain centered and calm.

I remain centered and calm in the midst of outer confusion/turmoil.

I touch into the peace within.

I observe myself from my center.

I remain in my center as the objective observer.

My center provides a safe, comfortable place from which to observe.

I feel one with myself, my Oversoul, and God while in my center.

CHANGE

I move through my fear of the unknown.

I am comfortable in the midst of my discomfort.

I am willing to release the old.

I easily accept and implement the new.

I am flexible.

Change is possible.

Change is acceptable.

I enjoy the challenge of change.

HABIT RESPONSES

I release the need for all old, unnecessary habit responses.

I choose my own actions and reactions.

I always have a choice.

I stop and think before I react.

I assume responsibility for my thoughts, words, and deeds.

I choose habit responses that recreate my life in a positive way.

ILLUSION

I release the illusion of who I am.

I accept the reality of who I am.

I expand my definition of self.

I accept reality in exchange for illusion.

I penetrate the layers of illusion.

I release self-imposed limitations.

I release memories that keep me in illusion.

I move through and beyond illusion.

I allow reality to explain.

KNOWLEDGE

I move forward into "new" knowledge.

I ask for the wisdom to use all knowledge correctly.

I accept responsibility for deeper inner knowledge.

OBJECTIVE LISTENING

I objectively listen to myself.

I release words that weaken body, mind, or spirit.

I choose words that affirm the positive in my life.

I match feelings with words.

I listen through my Oversoul.

I am open and receptive to all levels of listening.

I move into continually deeper levels of inner listening.

OBJECTIVE OBSERVING

I observe myself in conscious awareness.

I observe myself without judgment or criticism.

I release the need to judge and criticize self.

I release the parts of myself that I no longer need.

I appreciate who I am and the learning that brought me here.

I am honest with myself.

I accept myself exactly as I am.

I respect myself.

I release the need to judge and criticize the outer world.

I accept the outer world as is.

I ask my Oversoul to explain the outer world.

I respect the outer world.

SPENDING ENERGY

I organize my energy in conscious awareness.

I spend my energy efficiently.

I stop and think before I speak or act.

I use universal energy to make specific choices quickly.

VERTICAL EXPERIENCES

I release the need for horizontal experiences.

I choose vertical experiences.

I choose vertical experiences to accelerate my inner growth.

I move my psychic energy up instead of out.

I extract all knowledge available from every experience.

I allow vertical experiences to move me through illusion.

MEDITATIONS

MOVE DEEP WITHIN YOUR CENTER

Follow your breath deep within your center.

With each breath in, silently say "deeper".

With each breath out, silently say "deeper".

Feel yourself sink into continually deeper levels of silence.

Feel the peace and comfort that exists within the depths of your being.

Recognize that you feel safe and secure within your center.

Feel the connection that already exists between yourself, your Oversoul, and God.

Recognize that their strength is your strength.

Know that as long as you remain in your center, you can observe whatever you need to observe without discomfort.

In the same way, know that the turbulence of the outer world can circulate all around you without pulling you into it as long as you remain in your center.

Release all your feelings up to your Oversoul. Give thanks for the knowledge.

LISTEN TO YOUR VIBRATORY IMPRINTS

Ask your Oversoul to help you listen to the experiences that are contained in your vibratory imprints.

Follow your breath deep within.

With every breath, feel yourself sink deeper and deeper within.

Feel the inner connection between yourself, your Oversoul, and God.

Listen.

Do not *expect* anything; allow whatever happens to happen.

MEDITATION PRAYER FOR CHANGE

As you follow your breath deep within, use the following prayer.

Divine Mother, Holy Father;

Thank you for all that I have and all that I receive. Thank you for all my challenges. I accept them as the learning tools that they are. I only ask that you explain them to me so that I can understand the learning that they bring. For this reason, I offer them back to you.

I am willing to release them to you permanently so that I may grow into new avenues of awareness. I am willing to explore any options that you present to me. I am willing to accept any people or challenges that you choose to put before me. I only ask that you explain so that I may understand.

(Remain in your center. Listen to the silence.)

For this learning and the knowledge that it contains, I give thanks in your name. Amen.

RELEASING MEDITATION

Without labeling specific areas, ask that all unnecessary patterns, habit responses, and vibratory imprints be released from your life. Using your breath, breathe in the new from your Oversoul through the top of your head to the base of your spine. Observe that it is clear and clean.

Breathing out in reverse order, release the old. Observe that it is dark and heavy. When you are through, observe how you feel. Release those feelings up to your Oversoul. Give thanks for the releasing process.

RELEASING HABIT RESPONSES

Your habit responses are interconnected. Deciding to change one instigates a chain reaction in many areas. In conscious awareness, determine those areas to accelerate the change.

For example, you decide that irritation is a habit response. Ask your Oversoul to show you all the places in your life where irritation exists. Release those feelings up to your Oversoul. Continue to trace irritation feelings back through your life as far as possible.

Every time you release those feelings, the habit response of irritation weakens. Eventually, you will begin to notice that the outer world tends to irritate you less and less. The uncomfortable feelings that have lived within took up space. Releasing them allows room for comfortable feelings to exist.

RELEASING UNCOMPLETED EXPERIENCES

Choose an experience that has remained with you through the years that you would like to "forget".

Breathe yourself into your center.

As an objective observer, allow the experience to rise before your inner eye.

Observe the emotions that you feel. Allow the part of you that contains those emotions to yell, scream, cry, or do whatever it needs to do to cleanse itself.

Observe this part of yourself expressing to your Oversoul exactly how it feels. Ask your Oversoul to pass this message on to all other involved Oversouls. Ask that these Oversouls pass the message on to the involved individuals.

Release everything up to your Oversoul as it occurs. Acknowledge your learning from the experience. Observe how you feel after releasing it. Give thanks for the experience and complete your meditation.

MEDITATION PRAYER FOR INNER HARMONY

Use the following prayer to acknowledge the inner work that you are doing.

Divine Mother, Holy Father;

Thank you for all the tools that you have given me to help me learn and grow. All I have to do is breathe myself into my center and you are there. Acknowledging your strength acknowledges my strength. Remaining in my center, I feel and understand your vastness. At the same time, I understand my own vastness.

As with you, I understand that I am neither positive nor negative, but contain both. I know that each explains a part of myself. And every part of me exists for a purpose. As I release the turbulent parts with understanding, I move closer to the peaceful parts. In the end, they are all one and the same. They are all a part of me, and all a part of you.

I am discovering that I like myself. I like who and what I am. I appreciate the experiences that have brought me to this point in time. And better still, I understand these experiences. Moving through the illusion of turbulence has taken me into the reality of the deep inner peace which already exists within. All I have to do is to let go and let God.

For this knowledge and these experiences, I give thanks in your name. Amen.

MEDITATION REVIEW

Take a few moments to review your meditation time. Breathe yourself into your center and evaluate your accomplishments. Use the following questions as a guideline:

Is your meditation time worthwhile?

What are you accomplishing?

Is your body more relaxed than when you first began?

Does your breathing pull you into your center?

Are you moving into deeper levels of inner awareness?

Are you touching into a place of inner peace?

Are you cultivating skills that you can use throughout the day?

Are you able to observe and listen to yourself objectively?

Are you less judgmental and critical of yourself?

Are you finding out who you are?

Compared to when you first started meditating, where are you now?

Is your meditation time worthwhile? Only you know.

GLOSSARY

GLOSSARY

AURA: Your personal energy field.

AFFIRMATION: A statement in the present tense that defines a course of action, or a state of inner being. It is repeated many times by thinking, speaking, or writing it to bring new avenues of action into your conscious mind.

CENTER: Your center is aligned along your spine. It provides a safe space from which to work. You pull yourself into it by willing yourself into it.

COLLECTIVE CONSCIOUS MIND: The body of space that contains the accumulated known knowledge of humankind.

COLLECTIVE UNCONSCIOUS: The body of space that contains the accumulated thoughts of humankind. These established thought patterns directly affect what you are moving through today.

CONSCIOUS MIND: Contains your present.

DIRECT AWARENESS: To know by experiencing the knowledge.

GOD: Neutral energy. All that is.

HABIT RESPONSE: An established pattern of behavior that allows you to react to any given situation without thinking. Whether physical or mental, it can be positive, negative, or neutral.

HORIZONTAL EXPERIENCE: Pulls you out into similar growth.

ILLUSION: The way you perceive things to be.

KARMA, LAW OF: The natural process of balance that maintains your identity as individualized neutral energy.

KARMIC BOND: An agreement on the inner levels between one or more persons, or life forms. It allows each participant to understand the full spectrum of a single experience to maintain his/her identity as individualized neutral energy.

KNOW BY KNOWING: To know through direct awareness. To understand the feeling of an experience.

KNOWLEDGE: Information.

MACROCOSM: God. The universe.

MEDITATION: A process that moves you beyond words and connects you with silence, the level of feeling.

MICROCOSM: You. A world in miniature.

NEGATIVE: Negative is not "bad". It is merely a condition that exists.

OBJECTIVE LISTENING: Listening and evaluating without judgment or criticism.

OBJECTIVE OBSERVING: Watching and evaluating without judgment or criticism.

OVERSOUL: Neutral energy that comes out of God. Your Oversoul is to you what your Earth parents are to your body.

PSYCHIC ENERGY: Your personal energy. It flows back and forth and is horizontal.

POSITIVE: Positive is not better than negative. It is merely a condition that exists.

REALITY: The way things really are. It may vary considerably from your perception of the way you think things are.

SILENCE: The deepest level of inner awareness. The level of feeling. You connect with your Oversoul and God within silence.

SPIRITUALITY: A state of inner being.

SUBCONSCIOUS MIND: Contains your memories, moment by moment, lifetime by lifetime.

SUPERCONSCIOUS MIND: Provides the direct link to your Oversoul and God.

UNIVERSAL ENERGY: Energy that is available to everyone. Using it allows you to keep your psychic energy. It flows up and down and is vertical.

VERTICAL EXPERIENCE: Pulls you up into new growth.

VIBRATORY IMPRINT: Accumulated feelings of like experiences. They cause you to react to your experiences of today through your accumulated feelings of yesterday.

WISDOM: Knowledge applied.

YOU: Individualized neutral energy.

INDEX

INDEX

T

Talk, talking 41, 46, 51, 60 - 61, 66
Task 96 - 97
Taste buds 110
Tastes 35
Teamwork 77
Techniques 133 - 134
Teen 86
Telephone 18
Television 18
Tension 67, 97 - 98, 104, 124
Test 43
Theologians 75 - 77
Theories 134
Think 42, 44
Thought 32 - 33, 60 - 61, 66, 73, 76, 80, 97, 103, 115, 120, 123
    energy 60 - 61
Threat, threaten 52, 59
Time 17, 25, 28, 30, 32, 35, 54 - 55, 57, 61, 66 - 69, 73, 76 - 77, 81 - 82, 88 - 89, 92, 95 - 96, 98, 101 - 102, 104, 108 - 109, 117, 123, 126, 134
    frame 73
    period 95, 97
Tired 97
Today 40
Tone 38
    of voice 34 - 35, 37, 41 -

42, 49
Tools 33, 74, 100, 102 - 103, 107 - 108, 112, 134
Touches 35
Toxins 111
Transition 117
    period 57
Transmission of sound waves 18
Transportation 121
Tree 91
Trial and error 18
Trust 49
Truth 46, 81, 103
Try, trying 38, 56 - 58, 76, 86, 108, 116, 120

U

Uncomfortable 27, 59, 107
Unconscious 34, 43
    reaction 59
Understand 35, 38, 53
Unfamiliar territory 51, 59, 107
Unhealthy 111
Universal energy 45, 103
Universe 101
Unknown 53, 77
Unnecessary foods 111
    vibratory imprints 111
Unravel 21
Unresolved memories 79

ORDERING INFORMATION

For additional copies of

IN SEARCH OF YOURSELF: The Beginning

or

IN SEARCH OF YOURSELF: Moving Forward

please enclose $10.00 per book plus $1.50 shipping and handling for the first book and $1.00 shipping and handling for each additional book within the continental U.S.A.

International orders enclose $2.00 shipping and handling book rate (allow 8-10 weeks delivery) or $5.00 shipping and handling air mail.

Washington state residents add .075 sales tax.
All prices U.S. currency.

Send orders to:

Expansions Publishing Company, Inc.
P. O. Box 1360
Ellensburg, WA   98926
U.S.A.

Allow 2-4 weeks for delivery.

Notes

Notes

Notes

Notes

Notes